CADOGAN CHESS BOOKS

Garry Kasparov's
Chess Puzzle Book

CADOGAN CHESS BOOKS

Chief Advisor: Garry Kasparov
Editor: Andrew Kinsman
Russian Series Editor: Ken Neat

Other titles in this series include:

AVERBAKH, Y.
Chess Endings: Essential Knowledge

GELLER, Y.
The Application of Chess Theory

KASPAROV, G. et al.
Kasparov: The Ultimate Grandmaster

LIVSHITZ, A.
Test Your Chess IQ Books 1-3

NEISHTADT, I.
Queen Sacrifice

POLUGAYEVSKY, L.
Grandmaster Achievement

POLUGAYEVSKY, L.
Grandmaster Performance

POLUGAYEVSKY, L.
The Sicilian Labyrinth Vols. 1 & 2

POLUGAYEVSKY, L.
& DAMSKY, I.
The Art of Defence in Chess

SHEKHTMAN, E. (Compiler)
The Games of Tigran Petrosian
Vols. 1 & 2

SHERESHEVSKY, M.
Endgame Strategy

SHERESHEVSKY, M.
& SLUTSKY, L.
Mastering the Endgame Vols. 1 & 2

SMYSLOV, V.
Smyslov's 125 Selected Games

TAL, M. & DAMSKY, I.
Attack with Mikhail Tal

VAINSTEIN, B.
David Bronstein: Chess Improviser

For a complete catalogue of CADOGAN CHESS books (which includes the former Pergamon Chess and Maxwell Macmillan Chess list) please write to:

Cadogan Books, London House, Parkgate Road, London SW11 4NQ
Tel: (0171) 738 1961
Fax: (0171) 924 5491

Garry Kasparov's Chess Puzzle Book

by

Garry Kasparov

Translated and Edited by Ken Neat

CADOGAN CHESS
LONDON, NEW YORK

CADOGAN BOOKS DISTRIBUTION

UK/EUROPE/AUSTRALASIA/AFRICA
Distribution: Grantham Book Services Ltd, Isaac Newton Way,
Alma Park Industrial Estate, Grantham, Lincs NG31 9SD
Tel: 0476 67421; Fax: 0476 590223

USA/CANADA/LATIN AMERICA/JAPAN
Distribution: Paramount Distribution Center, Front and Brown Streets,
Riverside, New Jersey 08075, USA
Tel: (609) 461 6500; Fax: (609) 764 9122

English Translation Copyright © 1995 Ken Neat

First published 1995 by Cadogan Books plc, London House, Parkgate Road,
London SW11 4NQ

British Library Cataloguing in Publication Data
A CIP catalogue record for this book is available from the British Library

ISBN 1 85744 140 0

Cover design by Brian Robins

Typeset by Ken Neat, Durham

Printed in Great Britain by BPC Wheatons Ltd, Exeter

Contents

Introduction

The complexity of a chess game is largely determined by the dynamism of the positions arising. The growing professionalism of modern chess players allows them by prophylactic measures to exercise strict control over the play. To the forefront come elements such as logic and rationalism. But logic, defensive technique and deep theoretical knowledge in the opening are frequently insufficient for victory against an opponent of equal class. One way or another, a player is obliged deliberately to go in for a disturbance of the dynamic equilibrium. This is achieved by means of original strategical ideas, unexpected and at first sight paradoxical manoeuvres, and, of course, by means of sacrifices of material.

The tactical arsenal of the modern player is very wide and varied. Many typical combinations have been studied in detail and are confidently employed not only by professionals, but also by ordinary amateurs. And yet the value of a chess combination in the aesthetic sense remains unchanged, provoking a feeling of admiration and creative pleasure.

The value of each spectacular combination is high for the added reason that many players have mastered the technique of realising a slight material advantage. One always has to take into consideration that sacrificed pieces may be returned and play taken into a technically won ending, or a counter-attack launched.

This book contains the most interesting combinations from games played in 1993. Undoubtedly of particular interest are those that have occurred in games by supergrandmasters. As examples of these, we will first examine two games that are full of drama, and abound in tactical and combinational ideas, and in original strategical concepts.

Short-Kasparov
London 1993 (8th match game)

This is a position from a topical variation of the Sicilian Defence. White has a clear lead in development and is ready for an attack in the centre and on the kingside. If he can safeguard his king and include his rooks in the attack, Black's position will become critical. Playing such positions as Black demands not only great defensive skill, but also an ability to take unusual strategical decisions, based on precise tactical calculation. With his next few moves Black creates the preconditions for complications, in the hope of creating counterplay and seizing the initiative.

1...h5 2 ♕g3 h4 3 ♕g4 g5!?

Risky, but consistent.

4 0-0-0!

An excellent decision! White sacrifices a piece to gain a very strong attack. In such positions it is hardly necessary to work out all the possible variations – White's intuition will suggest to him that his attack is bound to be very dangerous.

4...♕e7?

Defending the e6 pawn. After 4...gxf4 5 ♘xe6 ♘xe6 6 ♗xe6 fxe6 7 ♕g6+ ♔e7 8 ♖d6 White would have gained a clear advantage, but stronger here is 6...♕e7 7 ♘d5 ♘xe5 8 ♘xe7 ♘xg4 9 ♗xc8 ♘f2 10 ♗b7 ♔xe7 11 ♗xa8 ♔f6 with approximate equality.

But Black also had at his disposal another excellent resource – 4...♖h6!, when White's attack becomes problematic.

5 ♘c6!!

White fully activates all his pieces and condemns Black, after a forced

variation, to a difficult defence.

5...♘xb3+ 6 axb3 ♕c5 7 ♘e4!

Much stronger than 7 ♘d4 gxf4 8 ♘xe6, although even in this case White has a dangerous attack.

7...♕xc6 8 ♗xg5 ♗b7

9 ♖d6!

A brilliant resource!

If now 9...♕xe4, then White wins by 10 ♖xe6+!, while after 9...♘xe5 he has the decisive 10 ♘f6+ ♔e7 11 ♖hd1! ♕xd6 12 ♖xd6 ♔xd6 13 ♕d4+ ♔c7 14 ♗f4! ♗d6 15 ♗xe5 ♗xe5 16 ♕xe5+, with a winning position.

9...♗xd6 10 ♘xd6+ ♔f8 11 ♖f1

Despite being a whole rook down, White has a very strong attack.

11...♘xe5 12 ♕xe6 ♕d5 13 ♖xf7+?

White's conduct of the attack has been inspired and highly spectacular, but here he makes a mistake. He could have won by 13 ♕f6! ♖h7 14 ♖f5! ♕xg2 15 ♕xe5 with the threats of ♗e7+ and ♖xf7+.

13...♘xf7

Of course, not 13...♚g8 on account of 14 ♖g7+! ♚xg7 15 ♘f5+ ♚f8 16 ♕e7+, and White wins.

14 ♗e7+ ♚g7 15 ♕f6+ ♚h7 16 ♘xf7 ♕h5!

17 ♘g5+ ♚g8 18 ♕e6+ ♚g7 19 ♕f6+ ♚g8 20 ♕e6+ ♚g7 21 ♗f6+ ♚h6 22 ♘f7+ ♚h7 23 ♘g5+

Repeating moves to gain time on the clock. In the event of 23 ♘xh8 ♖xh8 24 ♕e7+ ♚g6 25 ♗xh8 ♕h6+ 26 ♚b1 ♗xg2 Black would have saved the game.

23...♚h6 24 ♗xh8+

White again avoids the possible transition into an ending with opposite-colour bishops, rightly assuming that it does not promise a win – 24 ♕e7 ♖ag8! 25 ♘f7+ ♚g6 26 ♘xh8+ ♖xh8 27 ♗xh8 ♕g5+ 28 ♕xg5+ ♚xg5 29 g3 hxg3 30 hxg3 ♚g4 31 ♗e5 ♗d5! 32 ♚d2 ♚f3! 33 ♚d3 ♗e4+, and White is unable to create a second passed pawn. An almost study-like draw!

Short wants to decide the out-

come with a direct attack on the black king.

24...♕g6

The knight cannot be taken on account of mate.

25 ♘f7+ ♚h7 26 ♕e7

26...♕xg2?

This mistake could have had fatal consequences. Stronger was 26...♚g8! 27 ♕xb7 ♖f8 28 ♘e5 ♖f1+ 29 ♚d2 ♕d6+, with chances of a successful defence.

27 ♗e5?

The tension and time trouble lead to both sides making mistakes. White could have won by 27 ♗d4!, restricting Black's heavy pieces. Now Black succeeds in saving the game.

27...♕f1+ 28 ♚d2 ♕f2+ 29 ♚d3

29 ♚c3 was risky in view of the possible 29...b4+ 30 ♚xb4? ♕b6+, although 30 ♚d3 still draws.

29...♕f3+ 30 ♚d2 ♕f2+

Draw agreed. A battle on a grand scale!

Kamsky–Karpov
Dortmund 1993

A typical Caro-Kann situation. White has a slight spatial advantage, while Black has a defensive, but strategically sound position. There is nothing to herald a sharp intensification of the struggle. Black's paradoxical decision is based on a concrete tactical idea – that of exploiting the unfortunate position of the white queen at h4. At the moment ...g7-g5 is not possible on account of ♗xg5, and Karpov makes a 'shocking' choice...

1...♔e7!!?

Black voluntarily deprives himself of the right to castle, but he now threatens ...g7-g5 and then ...e6-e5. Essentially Black draws the enemy fire, forcing White to go in for a sharpening of the position. Kamsky's decision to sacrifice a pawn and seize the initiative is logical and well-founded.

2 ♘e5 ♗xe5 3 dxe5 ♕a5+ 4 c3 ♕xe5+ 5 ♗e3 b6

Sounder than 5...c5 in view of the possible 6 0-0-0 g5 7 ♕g3! ♕xg3 8 hxg3, threatening simultaneous attacks on the c5 and g5 pawns.

6 0-0-0 g5 7 ♕a4

7 ♕h3 followed by ♖he1 also came into consideration, aiming for an attack in the centre.

7...c5 8 ♖he1 ♗d7 9 ♕a3 ♖hd8 10 g3

White has sufficient compensation for the sacrificed pawn – his pieces are active and well coordinated.

10...♕c7 11 ♗d4 ♗e8! 12 ♔b1 ♖d5 13 f4! ♖ad8 14 ♗c2! ♖5d6 15 ♗xf6+ ♔xf6 16 fxg5+ hxg5 17 ♖xd6 ♖xd6 18 c4

The position has simplified – Black has succeeded in avoiding a direct attack and in retaining his extra pawn, although the position of his king is insecure. Later both players made mistakes, but Black nevertheless succeeded in winning the game. It would seem that what particularly told on the result was the stunning psychological effect of the move 1...♔e7, which disturbed the usual logic of White's reasoning.

The main material of the book is arranged such that the reader can become better familiar with the tactical properties of each of the pieces. Each section is accompanied by special tests to develop combinational ability, and the solutions to these are given at the end of the book.

1   The Queen

The sacrifice of the strongest chess piece is especially highly ranked among chess combinations. The sacrifice of the queen certainly occurs much more rarely than combinations where other pieces are given up. 1993 saw several striking examples on this theme. The sacrifice of a queen normally crowns a combinational attack and leads to a rapid show-down.

I.Ivanov–Spasov
Sliven 1993

Black has succeeded in halting the advance of the white pawns on the kingside. The whole question for White is how to set them in motion, not forgetting about the safety of his own king.

1 ♖f6!

Practically sacrificing the queen, but preparing g5-g6 with decisive effect.

1...♖xh7 2 ♘h5!

The sacrifice cannot be accepted – 2...♖xh6 3 ♖xh6+ ♘h7 4 g6 with inevitable mate. From the practical point of view, Black's best chance now was 2...♕c3. White must reply accurately, since Black may gain counterplay after 3 ♖e2 ♕a1+ 4 ♔f2 ♕h1 or 4 ♔g2 ♕d1. Correct is 3 ♔f2! ♕xc2+ 4 ♖e2, retaining dangerous threats.

2...♕e7 3 ♖ef1

Everything is ready for the advance of the g-pawn.

3...♗d5 4 g6! ♘xg6 5 f8=♖+

Black resigns. White's queen and pawns performed splendidly in their 'kamikaze' role.

When solving the combinational test, the reader will already know that the theme of each position is a queen sacrifice. At the same time, all variations need to be calculated to the end. The optimal time to spend on the solving of this test is 35-40 minutes.

TEST 1
Positions 1-9

1

Zsu.Polgar–Smyslov
Vienna 1993
White to play

2

Chiburdanidze–Larsen
Vienna 1993
White to play

3

Karayannis–R.Bellin
1993
Black to play

4

Høi–Degerman
Denmark-Sweden 1993
White to play

5

Mestel–J.Polgar
Oviedo 1993
Black to play

6

Hjartarson–G.Georgadze
Tilburg 1993
Black to play

7

Grabuzova–Nunn
Pardubice 1993
White to play

8

J.Polgar–Fernandez Garcia
Dos Hermanas 1993
White to play

9
Karpov–Salov
Linares 1993
White to play

2   The Rook

The rook coordinates splendidly with all the other pieces, but for this it needs operational scope – open and half-open files. Quite often by means of a rook sacrifice the opponent's king can be drawn out of its shelter or lured onto a square where it comes under a mating attack.

Of course, the rook is seen in all its glory in rook endings, but in the middlegame too this piece is capable of displaying its great tactical power.

Berezjuk–Joecks
Erfurt 1993

White's heavy pieces are very active and better coordinated, and the black king's position is insecure. White succeeds in including all his pieces in the attack on the king, by means of a rook sacrifice.

1 ♖xh6+! gxh6

It is unfavourable to decline the sacrifice – 1...♔g8 2 ♕e6+ ♖f7 3 ♖h8+ ♔xh8 4 ♕xf7, and White retains a mating attack.

2 ♕xh6+ ♔g8 3 ♘d5 ♘e5

Black had a difficult choice, e.g.:

(a) 3...♖b6 4 ♘e7+ ♔f7 5 ♕h7+ ♕g7 6 ♕h5+ ♖g6 7 ♘xg6 ♕xg6 8 ♖e7+!;

(b) 3...♕g7 4 ♘e7+ ♔f7 5 ♕h5+ ♔f6 6 ♕f5 mate;

(c) 3...♕xd3 4 ♘e7+ ♔f7 5 ♕h5+ ♔g7 (5...♔f6 6 ♘d5+ ♔g7 7 ♖e7+) 6 ♕g4+ ♔h7 (6...♔h8 7 ♘g6+; 6...♔f7 7 ♘f5) 7 ♘f5! ♕xf5 (7...♖xf5 8 ♖e7+ ♔h6 9 ♕g7+ ♔h5 10 ♕h7+ ♔g5 11 ♕g8+ and mate next move) 8 ♖e7+ ♕f7 9 ♕xd7 ♖f2 (9...♕xe7 10 ♕xe7+ ♔g8 11 ♕g5+) 10 ♕xb7, with advantage.

Probably 3...♖xg2 was objectively best here, simplying after 4 ♘e7+ ♔f7 5 ♔xg2 ♕g7+ 6 ♕xg7+ ♔xg7 7 ♘d5, although the resulting ending is a technical win for White. But stronger is 5 ♕h7+ ♕g7 (5...♔f6 6 ♔xg2, or 5...♖g7 6 ♕h5+) 6 ♕h5+ ♖g6 7 ♕d5+ ♔e8 8 ♘c6+, with a winning attack.

Black is still hoping to repulse the attack.

4 ♘e7+ ♔f7 5 ♘f5! ♛c3 6 ♖f1!

White methodically builds up the pressure, since the opponent's king is helpless against the numerous threats.

Here **Black resigned**, a decision that was quite timely, e.g. 6...♖e8 7 ♛g7+ ♔e6 8 ♘d4+! ♛xd4 9 ♖f6 mate, or 6...♔e8 7 ♛e6+ ♔d8 8 ♛e7+ ♔c8 9 ♘d6+ and mate next move.

Fahnenschmidt–Stohl
Germany 1993

A typical situation – Black is a pawn up, but he is behind in development and has come under an attack in the centre. Before the black king slips away, White must open another attacking line. To his aid comes a pretty combinational blow.

1 ♖xe5+!!

Despite its obvious nature, this sacrifice demanded precise calculation.

On 1...♛xe5 White would have won by 2 ♗f4! ♛c5 3 ♛d8+ ♔f7 4 ♛c7+ (4 ♖d7+ ♘xd7 5 ♛xd7+ ♛e7 6 ♗e6+ ♔f8 7 ♗d6 ♖e8 8 ♛xb7! is also possible) 4...♛e7 (or 4...♘d7 5 ♗e6+!) 5 ♗e6+!, while if 1...♔f7 2 ♗e6+ ♔e8 3 ♗b3+ fxe5 4 ♛d8+ ♛xd8 5 ♖xd8 mate.

1...fxe5 2 ♗d8! ♛f7 3 ♛d6!

Total domination by the white pieces, with both ♗g5 and ♗e6 threatened. Black is in *zugzwang*.

3...b6 4 ♗g5 Black resigns

The white bishops are splendid – 4...♘a6 5 ♛d8+!, or 4...♛b7 5 ♛e6+.

Varejcko–Bonani
Cattolica 1993

For the sacrificed pawn White has gained obvious compensation in the activity of his pieces. Only the rook at f1 is unable for the moment to take part in tactical operations, but White quickly succeeds in solving this problem too. A basis for the start of the combination is also given by the fact that the black queen is undefined.

1 罝xe6!

Unexpected and spectacular: 1...fxe6 loses to 2 桌xe6+. White also gains a clear advantage after 1...罝xe6 2 豐xa8+ 罝e8 3 豐b7 or 3 豐xa7.

1...罝eb8

White appears to have miscalculated, but his concept is highly profound and original.

2 豐xf7+!

A blow of fearful strength. With this queen sacrifice White begins a direct mating attack.

However, there was also a simpler solution: 2 罝e8+! 罝xe8 3 桌xf7+ and 4 豐xb2.

2...垫xf7 3 罝xf6+ 垫e8 4 罝e1+ 垫d7 5 桌a4+ 垫c8?

If 5...垫c7 White wins by 6 罝e7+.

But 5...罝b5! was clearly a better defence, when White should still win, but not so simply.

6 罝e8+ 垫b7 7 罝e7+ 垫c8 8 罝c6+ 垫d8 9 罝xg7+ 垫e8 10 罝c8 mate!

Linovickij-Giharev
Correspondence 1992-3

This is a position from a topical variation of the French Defence. The white king appears less well protected than its opposite number. But White's pieces are better coordinated for attacking purposes, and this factor proves decisive.

1 罝xg7+!

Now the black king is obliged to embark on a 'journey' under the fire of the white pieces, since 1...包xg7 loses to 2 豐xh7+ 垫f7 3 桌g6+ 垫e7 4 豐h4+! and mate next move.

1...垫xg7 2 罝g1+ 垫f7

Black loses quickly after 2...垫h8 3 包g5 h6 4 桌xf5.

3 豐xh7+ 垫e8 4 桌xf5 cxd4

The only chance of creating counterplay. Black loses after either 4...罝xf5 5 罝g8+ 罝f8 6 豐g6+ 垫e7 7 豐g7+, or 4...exf5 5 罝g7 豐c7 6 包g5 豐c6 7 e6! 桌xe6 8 罝e7+ 垫d8 9 包xe6+.

5 包xd4 罝c8

The critical position. White needs to strengthen his attack, as well as to reckon with the opponent's counterplay. Everything rests on precise calculation.

6 罝g7! 罝xc3

This is stronger than 6...豐xc3+ 7 垫e2, when Black's counterplay peters out.

7 ♖e7+ ♚d8 8 ♖xd7+ ♚c8 9 ♕e7!

Now Black can give a discovered check, but this does not bring any real gains, e.g. 9...♖c7+ 10 ♚d1. And 9...♕xa3 does not help on account of 10 ♖d8+! (or 10 ♖c7+ ♚b8 11 ♖xb7+ ♚a8 12 ♖xa7+!, forcibly transposing into a won ending) 10...♖xd8 11 ♗xe6+ with mate to follow.

9...♖h8 10 ♗xe6 ♖xa3+ 11 ♚e2 ♕a6+ 12 ♚e1! ♕a5+ 13 ♚f1 ♕a6+ 14 ♘e2!

White could still have lost after 14 ♚g2 ♖g8+! 15 ♗xg8 ♕g6+ 16 ♚f1 ♖a1+ 17 ♚e2 ♕e4+. He would have had to play 15 ♕g7, with drawing chances.

But now **Black resigned**.

Lau–Lutz
Graz 1993

On even a brief glance at this position it is evident that the fate of the black king is unenviable. White finds a forced way to win.

1 ♖e7+! ♗xe7 2 ♕g7+ ♚e6

Or 2...♚e8 3 ♕xh8+ ♚d7 4 ♘xe7 ♚xe7 5 ♕xh7+ ♚d8 6 ♕xg6 with an easy win.

3 ♗d2!

The inclusion of the queen's rook in the attack is the quickest way to win, although White also has a clear advantage after 3 ♘xe7.

3...♖e8

3...gxf5 loses to 4 ♖e1+ ♚d7 5 ♖xe7+.

4 ♖e1+ ♚d7 5 ♘xe7 ♚d8 6 f5

Threatening to play the bishop to g5, as well as the further advance of this pawn.

But much stronger was the spectacular 6 ♘c6+! ♘xc6 (6...♕xc6 7 ♗a5+) 7 ♖xe8+, with an easy win.

6...♕xe7 7 ♖xe7 ♖xe7 8 ♗g5 ♖aa7 9 ♕f8+

Black resigns

Piket–Sosonko
Eindhoven 1993

A typical position with castling on opposite sides. It is the placing of the kings that acquires decisive significance. In search of counterplay, Black's pieces on the queenside have become cut off from their king and are unable to come to its aid. With a rook sacrifice White destroys the black king's pawn screen and begins a direct attack.

1 ♖xh7! ♔xh7

1...♗f5 2 ♘xf5 ♔xh7 3 ♖h1+ ♔g8 4 ♘h4 is little better for Black.

2 ♖h1+ ♔g7 3 ♖h6 ♖g8

Black loses after both 3...♗e8 4 ♘e6+ ♔g8 5 ♖xg6+ ♗xg6 6 ♕xg6+ ♔h8 7 ♘g5, and 3...♖xd4 4 ♕xg6+ ♔f8 5 ♖h8+ ♗xh8 6 ♗h6+, with inevitable mate.

4 ♖xg6+ ♔h8?!

Or 4...♔f8? 5 ♗h6+ ♗g7 6 ♖xg7 ♖xg7 7 ♕g6.

The best defence was 4...♔f7! 5 ♘e6!? ♖xg6 (5...♗xe6 is bad in

view of 6 dxe6+ ♔f8 7 ♕f5+ ♗f6 8 ♗h6+) 6 ♘d8+ ♔g7 7 ♘xb7 ♖xg3 with an unclear position, or 5 ♖xg8 ♔xg8 6 ♕g6+ ♔h8 7 ♕h6+ with a draw by perpetual check.

In the game Black defends badly.

5 ♖h6+ ♔g7 6 ♘e6+ ♗xe6 7 dxe6 ♔f8 8 ♕f5+ ♗f6?

8...♔e8 was stronger, although even this would not have saved the game – 9 ♕f7+ ♔d8 10 ♕xg8+ ♔c7 11 ♕f7.

9 ♕h5 Black resigns

Castro–Gamboa
Columbia 1993

Black's position looks sufficiently sound and promising – the extra white pawn does not make itself felt. At the same time White's pieces are very active, especially his rooks on the half-open files, and he makes excellent use of this factor to build up a swift attack.

1 ♖xb7!

Diverting the queen from the defence of the knight. Black is obliged to accept the sacrifice.

1...♕xb7 2 ♕xe5+ ♔g8

2...♔h7 is very strongly met by 3 h5, although the simple 3 ♕xc5 also ensures White a technically won position. With 2...♔g8 Black hopes to retain counterplay on the h-file.

3 ♖xf7!

Another spectacular rook strike, with which White forces a win.

3...♕xf7

On 3...♔xf7 White has the decisive 4 ♗e6+ ♔e7 5 ♗d5+!

4 ♗e6 ♖h7 5 ♗xf7+ ♖xf7 6 ♕xc5 ♖af8

Or 6...♖d8 7 ♕b6, and wins.

7 ♕xd4 Black resigns

The optimum time to be spent on each of the following three tests (Nos. 2-4) is 25-30 minutes.

TEST 2
Positions 10-17

10

Khenkin–Afek
Natanya 1993
White to play

11

Pelaez–De Dovitiis
Havana 1993
Black to play

12
Hess–Finegold
New York 1993
Black to play

13
Tolnai–Paschall
New York 1993
White to play

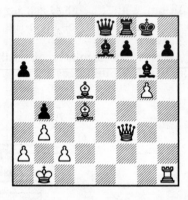

14
I.Ivanov–Mitkovsky
Sliven 1993
White to play

15
I.Sokolov–Mohr
Portoroz/Rogaska Slatina 1993
White to play

16

Van Wely–Berend
Brussels (Zonal) 1993
White to play

17

Cu. Hansen–Bagaturov
Biel 1993
White to play

TEST 3
Positions 18-23

18

Baburin–Adianto
Lichtenstein 1993
Black to play

19

Mellado–Pla
Seville 1993
White to play

20
Nenashev–Adianto
Asian Championship 1993
White to play

21
S.Guliev–Bologan
Ostrava 1993
Black to play

22
Winter–M.Ritova
Bad Wildbad 1993
White to play

23
Smyslov–Oll
Rostov 1993
White to play

TEST 4
Positions 24-30

24
Anand–Portisch
Biel 1993
White to play

25
Shirov–Chernin
Groningen 1993
White to play

26
Touzane–Kouatly
France 1993
White to play

27
Izeta–Vehi Bach
San Sebastian 1993
White to play

28
Gallagher–Koerant
Lyon 1993
White to play

29
Conquest–Bobzin
Bern 1993
White to play

30
Atlas–Wirthensohn
Switzerland 1993
White to play

3 Sacrifice of the Exchange

The sacrifice of a rook for a minor piece is nowadays a fairly trivial matter. The exchange sacrifice has essentially become a standard technique, and may be either intuitive, or based on precise calculation.

We recall standard exchange sacrifices by Black at c3 in the Sicilian Defence, at f3 in the French Defence, and so on. Usually such combinations serve as a prelude to the main idea of the attack.

In this chapter we will examine exchange sacrifices with the aim of obtaining an attack on the king.

Grigore–Holzke
Porz 1993

Material is roughly equal, but for the moment White's pieces are insufficiently well coordinated for an attack on the black king. With an excellent exchange sacrifice he includes his dark-square bishop, and creates a series of tactical threats.

1 ♖xd4! exd4

Black is forced to accept the sacrifice, since 1...bxc4 is very strongly met by 2 ♖d5!, e.g. 2...♕xa2 3 ♘xe5 ♘xe5 4 ♗xe5 ♗xe5 5 ♖xe5+ with a technically won ending, or 2...♕c7 3 ♖cd1! ♘b6 4 ♘xe5! ♘xd5 5 ♘xg6+ hxg6 6 ♗xc7.

2 ♗d6+ ♔e8

The only move, otherwise there is a forced mate after 2...♔f6 3 e5+ ♔f5 4 ♗d3+ ♔e6 5 ♘g5+ ♔d5 6 ♗e4.

3 ♗e6

White's minor pieces have splendidly woven a mating net.

3...♘b6

Or 3...♕a6 4 ♖c7.

4 b4!

Essential prophylaxis – if 4 ♖c7? ♕e1+ 5 ♔h2 ♗f8.

4...♕a3 5 ♖c7!

Threatening mate with the rook at e7.

5...♗f8

Or 5...♗f6 6 ♖b7.

6 ♘g5!!

Brilliant! White creates a new mating construction – 6...♗xd6 7 ♗f7+ and mate with the knight at e6.

6...♔d8 7 ♗f7!

A familiar idea – **Black resigns**.

Kveinys–D.Roos
Godesburg 1993

White's plans can only involve an attack on the kingside – Black has a dangerous passed pawn, which may decide the outcome. In addition, White's knight is attacked and he is threatened with the loss of the exchange. And yet he succeeds just in time in erecting a mating construction.

1 ♘e4! ♘e3+ 2 ♔e2 ♘xg4 3 ♕xg4 a3

Black exploits his main trump. Let us see whether he could have defended against the attack, without advancing his pawn. For example: 3...♕g7? 4 ♘f6+ ♔f8 5 ♕b4 mate. 3...♕h6 4 ♘f6+ ♔g7 is stronger. Here, as in the game, White could have played 5 h4, building up the threats, and all the same Black would have had to advance his a-pawn in search of counterplay.

4 ♘f6+ ♔g7 5 h4 a2 6 h5 a1=♕ 7 hxg6

The play is of a forcing nature. Despite his enormous material advantage, Black is unable to save his king from the mating attack.

7...♕xc3 8 ♘h5+ ♔g8 9 ♕g5!

The e5 pawn has to be defended. Now Black is helpless.

9...♕xd3+

Desperation, but Black has nothing better.

10 ♔xd3 ♖a3+ 11 ♔e2 ♕b4 12 ♘f6+

Mate is inevitable, and so **Black resigned**.

Landenbergue–Walther	Seirawan–Zarnicki
Switzerland 1993	*Buenos Aires 1993*

Black has played the opening badly and has come under a crushing attack. White could have won the exchange (the rook at h8) by 1 gxf7+, but he himself prefers to sacrifice the exchange, in order to create direct threats to the black king.

1 &xe6! &xh1 2 gxf7+ &d8

On 2...&e7? White would have won by 3 &d5+ &xd5 4 exd5.

3 &b6!!

Diverting the black queen from the defence of the d6 pawn.

3...&xb6 4 &xd6+!!

Another excellent blow – the point of the combination begun with 1 &xe6!

4...&xd6 5 f8=&+ &e8

Black can only play the dismal role of an onlooker.

6 &xd6+ &c7 7 &d5+ &b8 8 &xb6 &xg1+ 9 &d1 Black resigns

Another instant, and after castling the black king will safely escape from the centre. The position demands a vigorous decision. White, who has a lead in development, sacrifices the exchange to begin an attack.

1 &xd6! &xd6 2 &d1 &c7

2...&e7 is strongly met by 3 &e5.

3 &f4 &b7 4 &e5

White activates all his pieces and succeeds in coordinating them. It is difficult for Black to parry the direct threats.

4...&d7 5 &xd7!

Another thematic exchange sacrifice. It is now clear that a grim fate awaits the black king.

5...&xd7 6 &xc6 &a6 7 &xd7 &c8 8 &a4! &e7 9 &d3 f6

(*see diagram next page*)

10 ♕d6+ ♔f7 11 ♘e5+!
Vacating d7 for the bishop with gain of tempo. A spectacular, although simple knight sacrifice.

11...fxe5 12 ♗d7 ♕d8 13 ♕xe6+ ♔f8 14 ♗xe5 g6 15 ♗f6 **Black resigns**

For the solving of Test 5, 25-30 minutes are allowed.

TEST 5
Positions 31-37

31
Shmuter–Timoshenko
Nikolaev 1993
White to play

32
Ermenkov–Rasik
Budapest (Zonal) 1993
White to play

33
M.Gurevich–Prie
Clishy 1993
White to play

34
Adams–Stanton
London (Lloyds Bank) 1993
White to play

35
Lputian–Maahs
Antwerpen 1993
White to play

36
Okrajek–Magerramov
Bad Wörishofen 1993
Black to play

37

Shirov–Ivanchuk
Linares 1993
Black to play

4 The Bishop Sacrifice

In its long-range power a bishop is frequently not inferior to a rook. It is this long range that enables it to prepare an attack in leisurely fashion, imperceptibly. Even when a bishop is on its initial square, it can quickly and effectively join an attack or strike a tactical blow.

A bishop is especially dangerous in combination with a queen: the diagonal battery of these two pieces has destroyed many a king's fortress. At the same time, a bishop is a somewhat straightforward piece, and therefore fairly predictable in its actions.

In this chapter you will encounter a number of examples where a bishop is used for the destruction of the enemy king's pawn screen – by thematic sacrifices at h6 or h7. Often the f7 and g7 pawns also provide targets for combinational blows by bishops.

Of all the combinations begun with a bishop in games from 1993, the following must be considered the most spectacular.

Dolmatov–Razuvayev
Rostov 1993

White is a pawn up, but his king-side is somewhat weakened, and the black minor pieces are active. With his very next, ultra-spectacular move, Black gives the position a clear evaluation.

1...♗d4+!!

Into an attack by four pieces and the c3 pawn! White's reply is forced.

2 ♖xd4 ♘f3+ 3 ♔g2 ♘xd4 4 ♕xe6+

Transposing into an ending. Weaker is 4 ♕xd4 ♕xb3, when Black has a clear advantage.

4...♘xe6 5 ♖d1 ♖ae8

White has some compensation for the lost exchange, but it is obvious that the position favours Black.

Nadanian–Martirosian
Armenia 1993

The standard bishop sacrifice at h7 suggests itself, but in the given instance it is by no means trivial – Black has considerable defensive resources, and for the moment White's queen is not very well placed for the attack.

1 ♗xh7+ ♔xh7 2 ♘g5+ ♔g6

If 2...♔g8 White wins by 3 ♕h3.

3 f5+!

White opens the f-file and activates all his pieces.

3...exf5

3...♔xf5 is bad on account of 4 ♖hf1+ ♔g6 5 ♘f4+ ♔h6 6 ♕h3+ ♔xg5 7 ♕h5 mate.

4 ♘f4+! ♔xg5

The only move, since 4...♔h6 is decisively met by 5 ♕g3!

5 ♕g3+

5 ♘e6+ would also have won by force: 5...♔h5 6 ♕f3+ ♔g6 7 ♕g3+

♔h5 8 ♘xg7+ ♔h6 9 ♘xf5+ ♔h5 10 ♕f3+ ♔g6 11 ♘xe7+ ♘xe7 12 ♕f6+.

5...♔h6 6 ♕h3+ ♔g5 7 ♕h5+!

Drawing the black king into a mating net.

7...♔xf4

8 ♖he1!

Otherwise the black king would escape from the checks by capturing the e5 pawn. Now 9 g3 mate is threatened.

8...♘e4 9 ♖xd5 ♘xe5 10 ♖f1+ ♘f2

Or 10...♔e3 11 ♖f3+ ♔e2 12 ♖xf5+ ♔e3 13 ♖f3+ with an easy win.

11 ♖xf2+ ♔e4 12 ♖d1

Threatening to give mate by 13 ♕e2.

12...♘g4

12...f4 allows an attractive mate by 13 ♖e2.

13 ♕xf5+ Black resigns

Damaso–Arlandi
Lisbon 1993

White's combination is obvious – his bishops are trained on the kingside, and his queen and rook are ready to quickly join the attack.

1 ♗xh7+! ♔xh7 2 ♕xf7 ♗g5

Defending against the mate at g7 and against the rook check at h3.

3 ♖h3+ ♗h6 4 ♕f5+ ♔g8

The only move; after 4...g6 5 ♖xh6+ ♔xh6 6 ♕h3+ ♔g5 7 f4+ Black is mated.

5 ♕g6 ♔f8

5...♕f7 loses to 6 ♖xh6.

6 ♖xh6! gxh6 7 ♘f4

(*see diagram next column*)

7...♔e7!?

An attempt to slip away with the king to the queenside. It is difficult to suggest anything else.

8 f3 ♔d8 9 fxe4 dxe4 10 ♖c1

White brings his last reserve into the attack. **Black resigns**.

Kamsky–Lautier
Dortmund 1993

An open, dynamic struggle is in progress – the herald of piece attacks and combinational blows. White's queen/bishop battery is trained on the kingside, and the sacrifice of the dark-square bishop suggests itself. Nevertheless, White's attack is most probably of an intuitive nature.

1 ♗xh6! gxh6 2 ♕xh6 ♖e8

Vacating the f8 square for the bishop, which is needed for the defence.

At the same time, 2...♕b6 came into consideration, with the intention after 3 ♖fe1 ♕xf2+! 4 ♔xf2 ♘g4+ 5 ♔f1 ♘xh6 6 ♖xe7 of taking play into an ending, where Black would have retained practical drawing chances.

White would have had to play 3 ♘d5!? ♗xd5 4 ♗h7+! ♘xh7 (4... ♔h8 5 ♗f5+ ♔g8 6 ♖d3 and wins) 5 ♕xb6, with advantage.

3 ♗c4!

Retraining onto the f7 pawn and creating the threat of ♕g6+. 3 ♗f5 was weaker on account of 3...♕a5! 4 ♕g5+ ♔f8 5 ♖d3 ♘g8, when White's attack comes to a halt.

3...♗d7 4 ♖d4! ♗f8 5 ♕g6+ ♗g7 6 ♕xf7+ ♔h8 7 ♖h4+ ♘h7

8 ♖xh7+! ♔xh7 9 ♕h5+ ♗h6 10 ♗d3+ ♔g8 11 ♕xh6

Black resigns, without waiting for the dismal finish.

White's pieces are slightly more actively placed, but no direct threats are evident. He decides to sacrifice his bishop, to break up the king's pawn screen. The combination looks tempting, but Black finds adequate defensive resources.

1 ♗xh6!? gxh6 2 ♕xh6

Threatening ♘g5 and the switching of one of the rooks to the kingside.

2...♘6h7 3 ♗xf7+

This second bishop sacrifice is needed to develop the attack.

3...♔xf7 4 ♖xd7!

Very spectacular, but, unfortunately, it does not give White a decisive advantage.

4...♘xd7

Of course, not 4...♕xd7 5 ♘xe5+.

5 ♕xh7+ ♔f8

5...♔e6 loses to 6 ♕f5+ ♔d6 7 ♖d1+ ♔c5 8 ♖xd7 ♕b8 9 ♘xe5.

6 ♕h6+ Draw agreed

Komliakov–Gadzhily *Nikolaev 1993*	Serper–Nikolaidis *St. Petersburg 1993*

All White's pieces, with the exception of his light-square bishop, are aimed at the opponent's kingside. The sacrifice at h6 suggests itself, and after it all the remaining pieces take a direct part in the attack on the black king.

1 ♗xh6! gxh6 2 ♖xh6+ ♘xh6 3 ♕xh6+ ♔g8 4 ♗c4!

The light-square bishop too has become terribly strong.

4...♘e6

The a2-g8 diagonal has to be blocked.

Black would have lost quickly after 4...♔f7 5 ♘c7+ ♘e6 6 ♕h7 mate, or 4...♖f7 5 ♘xf6+ ♗xf6 6 ♖xf6 with crushing threats.

5 ♕g6+ ♔h8 6 ♖f3 ♘g5 7 ♖h3+!

Black resigns, in view of the inevitable mate after 7...♘xh3 8 ♕h6+ ♔g8 9 ♘xf6+.

In the opening White sacrificed a knight in return for a dangerous pair of connected passed pawns and a lead in development. The position of the black king in the centre also gives him additional tactical possibilities.

1 ♗b5!!

With this forcing move White begins an attack in the centre and on the queenside.

1...axb5 2 axb5 ♕xb5

Otherwise the pawn trio would have completed its destructive advance: 2...♕b7 3 c6 ♕b8 4 b6 – a unique position!

3 ♖xa8 ♕c6 4 ♖fa1

This rook is aiming for a7.

4...f4 5 ♖1a7!

White is ready to make further sacrifices. On 5...fxe3 he had prepared the spectacular 6 ♕d5! exf2+ 7 ♔xf2 with inevitable mate.

5...♘d7 6 ♖xc8+! (not allowing Black a moment's respite) **6...♕xc8**

7 ♕d5! fxe3 8 ♕e6+ ♔f8 9 ♖xd7 exf2+ 10 ♔f1! ♕e8

Black would also have lost after 10...♘g3+ 11 hxg3 ♕xd7 12 ♕xd7 hxg3 13 ♕e7+ ♔g8 14 ♕e8+ ♗f8 15 ♕xg6+ ♗g7 16 ♕xg3.

The following variation is very interesting: 10...♕a6+ 11 ♔xf2 ♕e2+! 12 ♔xe2 ♘f4+ 13 ♔f1 ♘xe6 14 c6 when, despite his two extra pieces, Black is helpless.

11 ♖f7+!!

White's conduct of the attack is inspired! Nevertheless he could also have chosen the fairly simple 11 ♕xe8+ ♔xe8 12 ♖e7+ ♔d8 13 c6 ♘g3+!? 14 hxg3 (14 ♔xf2 ♘f5!) 14...hxg3 15 ♔e2! ♖h1 16 c7+ ♔c8 17 ♖e8+ ♔b7 18 c8=♕+, with inevitable mate.

11...♕xf7 12 ♕c8+ ♕e8 13 d7!

This pawn has fulfilled its mission, and now it is the turn of the c-pawn.

13...♔f7 14 dxe8=♕+ ♖xe8 15 ♕b7+ ♖e7 16 c6! e4!

The last spark of Black's counterplay.

17 c7 e3 18 ♕d5+ ♔f6 19 ♕d6+ ♔f7 20 ♕d5+

Gaining time on the clock before the control – it is clear that White is going to take the rook with his queen.

20...♔f6 21 ♕d6+ ♔f7 22 ♕xe7+ ♔xe7 23 c8=♕ ♗h6 24 ♕c5+ ♔e8 25 ♕b5+ ♔d8 26 ♕b6+ ♔d7 27 ♕xg6 e2+ 28 ♔xf2 ♗e3+ 29 ♔e1

Black resigns. This was undoubtedly one of the most interesting games played in 1993.

Smirin–Kurajica
Zagreb 1993

At first sight the play seems of a strategical nature – White has set up a pawn blockade in the centre and is attempting to exploit the weakness of the dark squares on the queenside. Black's kingside is defended by a solid line of pawns. But White has noticed an important tactical detail –

the cramped position of the black queen and the weakness of the d7 pawn. This allows him to begin a massed attack over the entire board.

1 ♗xf5!

Threatening 2 ♖xd7, trapping the queen.

1...♘xe5

A counter-sacrifice, on which Black was evidently pinning great hopes. Had he anticipated the further development of events, he would possibly have preferred the modest 1...♗c8, which after 2 ♘xc8 ♖fxc8 3 ♗e4 a4 4 ♘c5 ♗xc5 5 ♗xc5 ♕a5 would at least have left him with some hopes of saving the game.

2 ♖xd7!

Nevertheless this blow takes place.

2...♘xd7 3 ♗xe6+ ♖f7

In any event White would have regained the sacrificed exchange.

4 ♘xd7 a4

A last attempt to gain counterplay. 4...♖e8 would have been strongly met by 5 ♗b6! ♕d6 6 ♖d1, while

the black queen is also unable to find a secure post after 5...♕c6 6 ♘xa5.

5 ♘bc5 ♗xc5 6 ♗xc5

The white pieces have generated enormous activity.

6...♖a8 7 ♗xf7+ ♘xf7 8 ♕e7 ♖c8 9 ♖e1

9...b3?

Overlooking the direct mating attack, but after the best move 9...h5 White also wins easily – 10 ♘f6+ ♔h8 11 ♕xc7 ♖xc7 12 ♗xb4.

10 ♕e8+!

Simply and elegantly forcing mate. **Black resigns** in view of 10... ♖xe8 11 ♖xe8+ ♔g7 12 ♗f8+ ♔g8 13 ♗h6 mate.

Psakhis–Lev
Herzliya 1993

White has an obvious advantage: his pieces are active and well coordinated. Black's kingside and his e7 pawn are weak, and he can only hope to save the game by going into an ending or by transferring his knight to e5.

1 ♗xg6!
Breaking up the pawn screen.
1...fxg6
If 1...♘e5 White wins by the simple retreat 2 ♗d3.
2 ♖xe7 ♘e5 3 ♖1xe5
The immediate 3 ♕h4 was also possible, and looks more decisive.
3...dxe5 4 ♕h4 ♕b6+ 5 ♔h2 ♔f8 6 ♖d7 Black resigns

For the solving of each of these tests (Nos. 6 to 8) 35-40 minutes are allowed.

TEST 6
Positions 38-43

38
Casella–Henao
New York 1993
White to play

39
Rolli–Hofmaer
1993
White to play

40
Zolnierowicz–Dokhoyan
Lublin 1993
Black to play

41
Lutz–Kuczynski
Germany 1993
White to play

42
Kuzmin–Akopian
Rostov 1993
Black to play

43
Skembris–Timman
Corfu (Match) 1993
White to play

TEST 7
Positions 44-49

44
Quillan–Levitt
British Championship 1993
White to play

45
Ulybin–Van Ryn
Leeuwarden 1993
White to play

46
Kosten–Mailfert
France 1993
White to play

47
Gazik–Chernin
Budapest (Zonal) 1993
Black to play

48
Sandqvist–L.Karlsson
1993
Black to play

49
Anand–Bareev
Linares 1993
White to play

TEST 8
Positions 50-55

50
Miles–Summerscale
Dublin (Zonal) 1993
White to play

51
Van der Sterren–Hort
Bern 1993
White to play

52
Orgovan–Rigo
Hungary 1993
White to play

53
I.Almasi–Videki
Kecskemet 1993
White to play

54
Ilincic–Makarov
Arandelovac 1993
Black to play

55
Ye Jiangchuan–Granda Zuniga
Biel (Interzonal) 1993
Black to play

5   Knight on the Attack!

The most distinctive chess piece, the knight is especially good in the middlegame, bringing to almost any position a degree of originality. A knight is very often sacrificed in order to open up the position and include the long-range pieces. The queen/knight duo is an ideal combination for attacking the king, and is capable of passing through practically any tactical labyrinth. Moreover, as a rule the knight prepares for the queen an invasion square or one on which it can land a decisive blow.

The participation of a knight in a combination always gives it a distinctive character. When playing Black in the Sicilian Defence, one must always be prepared for explosive attacks after knight sacrifices at b5 or d5. The appearance of a white knight at g5, or of a black one at g4, immediately creates dangerous threats to the opponent's king after kingside castling. Hence the aim to 'cripple' knights at the very start of the game, by pinning them with bishops.

But if a chess 'hussar' is free, it is capable of all kinds of feats, splendidly manoeuvring or participating in swift attacks. It is noteworthy that the greatest number of combinations given in this book are in some way or other associated with the tactical actions of knights.

A knight on the attack – this is always dangerous!

Dolmatov–Lutz
Germany 1993

White's heavy pieces and his two knights are well coordinated for an attack on the kingside. But the position must be opened up for the inclusion of the white bishops. With a blow by one his knights, White disrupts the harmony of the black pieces.

1 ♘3d4!

Threatening ♘xe6 and ♘xb5. Black is obliged to take the knight.

1...exd4 2 e5!

The light-square bishop joins the attack on the h7 pawn. White could have won the exchange by 2 ♘xd6 ♘e5 3 ♘xe8 ♖xe8, but then the black pieces would have been activated and the position would have become unclear. White's chief aim is an attack on the kingside.

2...♘xe5

The only move; 2...♗xe5 would have lost to 3 ♖xh7+! ♔xh7 4 ♘e7+.

3 ♖xh7+! ♔xh7?

After this White's combinational idea is fully justified. 3...♔g8! was much stronger. Events could then have developed according to the following scenario: 4 ♘h6+ ♔f8 5 ♖xf6+! ♔e7 6 ♖xg7+ ♔xf6 7 ♖xc7 ♗xc7 8 ♕h4+ ♔g7 9 ♘f5+ ♔f7. For the queen Black has gained sufficient material, and White does not appear to have any decisive threats.

4 ♘e7+!

White is only interested in an attack on the king – the regaining of the material does not attract him.

4...g6

Of course, not 4...d3 on account of mate by the queen at h4 or h3.

5 ♕h4+

The queen/knight duo goes into action. Much weaker was 5 ♗xg6+? ♔g7!, when the attack peters out.

5...♔g7 6 ♕xf6+ ♔h6 7 ♕h4+ ♔g7 8 ♕f6+ ♔h6

(*see diagram next column*)

9 ♘xg6!

The decisive blow, after which the black king is helpless, and attempts to somehow create counterplay are doomed to failure.

9...♗xg2+ 10 ♔xg2 ♘g4

10...♕c6+ 11 ♔g1 is also not dangerous for White.

11 ♕h4+ ♔g7 12 ♕xg4 ♘g5 13 ♕xd4+

The simplest: White forces a won ending.

13...♗e5 14 ♕xe5+ ♖xe5 15 ♗xe5+ Black resigns

Varga–Kustar
Budapest 1993

Combinations are normally begun with the most active pieces. In this case these are the queen and the two knights. The black bishops are inactive, and therefore the opening up of the position is in White's favour. Black's seemingly solid position collapses after a series of tactical blows.

1 ♘d5!

This knight leap into the centre is typical of Sicilian set-ups. The acceptance of the sacrifice loses quickly after 1...exd5 2 ♘f5 ♕f8 3 ♕g3.

Black can give up his queen for three minor pieces, but this too fails to save him – 1...♘xd4 2 ♘xe7 ♘xe2+ 3 ♔h1 ♔xe7 4 ♕d3, with a double attack on the knight and the d6 pawn.

1...♕d8 2 ♘xe6!

The white knights operate splendidly in the attack.

2...fxe6 3 ♕xe6+ ♔f8 4 ♗h5 ♘e5 5 ♘xb6!

Another diverting knight blow. 5...♕xb6 allows mate with the queen at e8, while on 5...♖c6 White has the decisive 6 ♖d5! ♖xb6 7 ♖xe5!

5...♕e7 6 ♖xd6

Coolly and strongly played. The exchange of queens does nothing to ease Black's defence.

6...♗xe4 7 f4 ♖c6

7...♕xe6 8 ♖xe6 ♘g6 9 ♘d7+ is no better.

8 ♖xc6

Black resigns (if 8...♘xc6 9 ♘d7+).

Haik–Gentilleau
Cannes 1993

At first sight White appears to have few grounds for a combination. Tactics such as ♖xd7 and ♘b6 do not achieve anything real, but merely simplify the position. He would like to exploit his heavy pieces on the f-file, but how to do this?

To the assistance come his knights, although their positioning on the edge of the board does not look very promising. But by means of a knight sacrifice White's position uncoils like a compressed spring.

1 ♘xg6!

White's combination is by no means an obvious one. It is only after a series of diverting blows that his pieces succeed in reaching the opponent's king.

1...fxg6 2 ♗xf4 exf4 3 ♕b3+!

For the moment the blows are from afar.

3...♔f8

3...♔h8 is strongly met by 4 ♕f7 (or 4 ♕h3+ ♔g8 5 ♖xd7), with the threats of ♖xd7 and ♖d3.

4 ♖xd7!

By this exchange sacrifice the black queen is diverted from the defence of the f4 pawn.

4...♕xd7 5 ♖xf4+ ♗f6 6 ♖xf6+ ♔g7 7 ♘c5!

This knight too offers itself, for the sake of a mating attack on the black king.

7...♕d4+

White has a technically won position after 7...♕c7 8 ♘e6+ ♖xe6 9 ♕xe6.

8 ♔h1 ♕xc5 9 ♖f7+ Black resigns

Howell–Ragozin
Cannes 1993

The g7 and h7 pawns are under fire from the white pieces, and it is clear that the main events will develop on the kingside. The showy ♕h6 is parried by the simple

...e6-e5. The transfer of the rook to h3 suggests itself – 1 ♖d3. In this case, of course, Black should not fall into the transparent trap 1...g6? 2 ♕xh7+!, but should play 1...bxc3 2 ♖h3 cxb2+ and then ...♕xe4, defending the h7 pawn. The tactical solution is provided by a thematic knight sacrifice.

1 ♘d5!

Spectacular and strong. White threatens ♘xe7+, and if the bishop moves he has the decisive 2 ♘f6+. Black is forced to accept the sacrifice, but now he will not have either ...e6-e5 or ...♕xe4.

1...exd5 2 ♖d3 ♖fc8 3 c3 dxe4 4 ♖h3 ♔f8

How is White to strengthen his attack? If 5 ♗xg7+ Black simply moves his king away to e8, and the same happens after 5 ♕xh7.

5 g6!

Also including the rook at g1 in the attack.

5...fxg6 6 ♕xh7 ♔e8 7 ♖xg6

The black pieces on the queenside do not manage to come to the aid of their king, and on the kingside White enjoys complete mastery.

7...♔d7 8 ♖xg7 ♖e8 9 ♗f6 ♕b5 10 c4

Depriving the opponent of the slightest saving hopes.

10...♕c6 11 ♖xe7+ ♖xe7 12 ♕xe7+ ♔c8 13 ♖h7

White can even permit himself this harmless 'joke', instead of the immediately winning 13 ♖h8+. **Black resigns**.

Tasic–G.Nikolic
Arandelovac 1993

The position in the centre has been opened to the advantage of White, whose pieces are clearly the more active. In addition the black king has not yet castled. With the aid of his knights, White succeeds in creating a splendid combination.

1 ♘e5!

1 ♕xb7? is much weaker on account of 1...0-0!, when, after safeguarding his king, Black can hope for counterplay.

1...♕h5

If 1...♕f5 White gains the advantage by 2 ♕xb7 0-0 3 ♘xc6, when 3...♗xe1 is not possible on account of 4 ♘e7+.

2 ♘xc6 ♗xe1 3 ♕c5!

The main target of the attack is the black king, which now, in view of the mate threat at e7, is forced to seek its own salvation.

3...♔d7 4 ♘e5+ ♔c8 5 ♘d6+ ♔b8

6 ♕c6!!

The crux of White's forcing combination. The queen cannot be taken on account of mate by the two knights, while 6...♗c8 is met by a no less spectacular queen sacrifice – 7 ♕xb7+! (7 ♘d7+ also mates, though less spectacularly), and mate with the knight at d7.

6...cxd6 7 ♕xd6+ ♔c8 8 ♕c5+ ♔b8 9 ♘d7+! ♗xd7 10 ♗f4+ Black resigns

Topalov–J.Polgar
Madrid 1993

White's pieces are the more active, especially his rook at h8, and he holds the initiative. But if he delays building up his attack, Black will gain counterplay.

Therefore he decides to sacrifice a knight at b5, especially since he obtains for it a sufficient pawn equivalent.

1 ♘dxb5! axb5 2 ♘xb5 ♕c6 3 ♘xd6+ ♚e7 4 fxe5 ♚e6

4...♘xe5 is unpleasantly met by 5 ♕b4!

Now it appears that White's attack has been halted, but there follows a new, far from obvious knight sacrifice, and again on the ill-fated (for Black) b5 square!

5 ♘b5! ♕xb5

Black is forced to accept the sacrifice, since 5...♕xe4 is bad on account of 6 ♘c7+, e.g. 6...♚e7 7 ♕d6+ ♚d8 8 ♖xf8 mate, 6...♚f5 7 ♕xd7+, or 6...♚xe5 7 ♗a7.

6 ♖xf8!

Threatening mate with the queen at d6.

6...♕c6 7 ♖xb8 ♘xb8 8 ♕d8

After the exchanges the position has markedly simplifed, but White still retains strong threats.

8...♘a6

The only square for the knight.

9 ♕f6+ ♚d7 10 ♕xf7+ ♚c8 11 ♕f8+ ♚c7 12 ♕f7+ ♚b8

13 e6!

This pawn finally decides the outcome.

13...♕xe4 14 e7 ♗c6 15 e8=♕+! Black resigns (15...♗xe8 16 ♕a7+ ♚c8 17 ♕xa6+ with an easy win).

Berzinsh–Patzl
Czechoslovakia 1993

It appears that White should be trying to exploit his pawn majority on the queenside, but it is not easy to effect a breakthrough here.

Black's kingside, protected by his line of pawns, looks impregnable, and yet it is here that White succeeds in mounting an attack with the help of a knight sacrifice. After this White's remaining pieces become very active, and the black king unexpectedly comes under a direct mating attack.

1 ♘dxf5! gxf5 2 ♘xf5 ♛d7 3 ♘h6+!

This is much stronger than 3 ♗xf6 ♛xf5 4 ♗xd8 ♖xd8, when Black has nothing to fear.

3...♔g7 4 ♗xf6+

The black king is very quickly drawn out of its seemingly secure shelter.

4...♔xf6 5 ♛d4+ ♔g6 6 f5+!

The decisive blow. The second knight is sacrificed, and in return White weaves a mating net.

6...♔xh6 7 ♛f6+ ♔g6 8 ♖xe4

Black resigns: after 8...♛xf5 White wins by 9 ♖h4+ ♛h5 10 ♖xh5+ ♔xh5 11 ♛h4 mate.

Dueball–Teske
Germany 1993

White has a clear advantage in the centre, and his pieces are the more active. Castling for Black involves a risk, since ...h7-h5 has already been played. All this creates the preconditions for a combinational attack.

1 ♘xe6!

By weakening the defences of the black king, and opening lines and diagonals, White sharply actives all his pieces. In the Sicilian Defence, when Black's bishop is at b7 his e6 pawn often becomes a target for tactical blows.

1...fxe6 2 e5 ♘g4

The opening of the d-file can only favour White, and also in this case his dark-square bishop is quickly included in the attack – 2...dxe5 3 fxe5.

3 ♗g6+ ♔e7 4 ♛e1!

Threatening to advance the queen to h4.

4...♘c5 5 b4!

White plays actively over the whole board.

5...♘a4 6 ♘xa4 bxa4 7 f5!

Not a moment's respite for the opponent! White now opens the central files for a direct attack on the king, at the same time activating his rook and dark-square bishop.

7...dxe5 8 ♗g5+ ♘f6 9 ♖d1

Now all White's pieces are participating in the attack.

9...♛c7 10 fxe6

Threatening 11 ♖d7+.

10...♚xe6 11 ♗f5+ ♚f7

12 ♗xf6 gxf6

If 12...♛c6 White would have won by 13 ♖d7+.

13 ♖d7+ ♛xd7 14 ♗xd7 ♖xc2 15 ♛xe5!

Black's temporary counterplay quickly peters out, and White continues his attack on the king.

15...♗xg2+ 16 ♚g1 ♗xf1 17 ♗e8+ ♚g8 18 ♛d5+ Black resigns

Tkachiev–Watson
London 1993

At first sight Black's position seems quite secure, but his queen is badly placed at c6, and his kingside is defended only by the dark-square bishop. This allows White to carry out a splendid attack, beginning with a knight sacrifice.

1 ♘d5! exd5 2 exd5 ♛d7

Other queen moves are no better.

3 ♗xf6 gxf6

This allows White to implement the main idea of the combination. Had Black foreseen the finish, he would no doubt have preferred the modest 3...♖e8, reconciling himself to a difficult defence after 4 ♖g3 g6.

4 ♖g3+ ♚h8

If 4...♚f8 White would have won by 5 ♛xh7 f5 6 ♖g8+ ♚e7 7 ♛h4+ f6 8 ♛h7 mate.

5 ♕xh7+!!

A brilliant strike, prepared well in advance.

5...♔xh7 6 ♖d4

With his enormous material advantage, Black has no defence against the mate. 6...♕h3!? is met by the simple 7 gxh3. **Black resigns**.

Khalifman–Kotronias
Belgrade 1993

Black is badly behind in development, and his pieces are cramped and inactive. White's pieces are concentrated in the centre and are excellently coordinated. In order to attack, he needs to open lines.

1 ♘f5! exf5 2 ♕f2 ♖e6 3 ♖xe6 ♕xe6

Forced, since if 3...fxe6 Black could have been unexpectedly mated after 4 ♗xh5+ ♔d8 5 ♕b6!

4 ♖e1 ♘f6 5 ♘d5!

White has no reason to hurry: he can calmly build up the threats.

5...♔d7 6 ♖xe6 fxe6

Nominally White has a slight material advantage, but in actual fact he has a continuing attack on the king.

7 ♘b6+ ♔c7

7...♔e8 is strongly met by 8 ♕d4!, when without loss of material Black cannot bring his pieces into play.

8 ♕e3!

This move achieves a more effective coordination with the knight and bishop.

8...♗d7 9 ♘c4 b6 10 ♕e5+ ♔c8 11 ♘d6+ ♗xd6 12 ♕xd6 ♘e4

Black has managed to avoid the direct attack, but the resulting ending is also hopeless.

13 ♗xe4 fxe4 14 ♔c1 e3 15 ♔d1 ♖b7 16 ♕f8+ Black resigns

Bologan–Nunn
Germany 1993

If the knight moves from g4, White will regain the e2 pawn and the position will become level. Is there any way of exploiting the temporary strength of the e2 pawn? To Black's aid comes a highly original combination, in which all his pieces participate.

1...♘b6!!

The second knight is also placed *en prise*! But in the first instance it was important for Black to move this knight away from the attack of the rook at d2.

The straightforward 1...♖f1+ 2 ♖xf1 e1=♕ would have given White the advantage after 3 ♖xd7! ♕xf1+ 4 ♔xf1 ♘h2+ 5 ♔g1 ♖xd7 6 ♔xh2.

2 ♖dxe2!

The only move. If 2 ♘xb6 Black would have replied with the spectacular 2...♖f1+! 3 ♖xf1 e1=♕ 4 ♖d3 ♕a5 5 ♘d5 ♖e1!

2...♖xe2 3 ♖xe2 ♘xc4 4 hxg4 ♘xb2 5 ♘d6 b6

Black has achieved an obvious advantage in the endgame – White's kingside pawns are weak.

Karpachev–Lyrberg
Gausdal 1993

White's queen and minor pieces are aimed at the opponent's weakened kingside, and his centralised rooks are ready to sacrifice themselves in order to achieve the main aim – an attack on the black king. It is hard to believe that within a few moves the game will be decided, but White's very first move, a knight sacrifice, signals the start of a direct attack.

1 ♘h5! gxh5

If 1...♗xh2+ the simple 2 ♔h1 is decisive. Black is forced to accept the sacrifice, otherwise White will set up a mating construction on the dark squares after ♘f6+.

2 ♖xe5!

By also sacrificing the exchange, White eliminates the main defender of the black king.

2...♘xe5

Of course, not 2...♕xe5 3 ♗f6, and wins.

3 ♗xh7+!

Very pretty – the third sacrifice in a row, and again Black is forced to accept it. If 3...♔g7, then 4 ♗f6+ ♔f8 5 ♕g5 wins.

3...♔xh7 4 ♕xh5+ ♔g8 5 ♗f6 ♘g4

It was possible to be mated a move later – 5...♘g6 6 ♕h6.

6 ♕h8 mate

Topalov–Gazik
Budapest 1993

The position is double-edged, but White's chances are better, since he has more pieces participating in the attack on the king. In the complications that now begin, a very precise calculation of the variations is demanded of both players. The start of the combination with a knight sacrifice only appears simple – in reality White burns his boats behind him, relying in particular on the activity of his queen and his rook at d6.

1 ♘f5+! ♗xf5 2 ♕xf6+ ♔g8 3 exf5 ♕a1+ 4 ♔d2 ♕xb2

The last chance – it is essential to maintain contact with the white king. Capturing the rook would have lost quickly: 4...♕xh1 5 fxg6 fxg6 6 ♕xg6+ ♔f8 7 ♖f6+ ♔e7 8 ♖f7+ ♔d8 9 ♕d6+, or 5...♖f8 6 gxf7+ ♖xf7 7 ♖d8+.

5 ♗d3!

A multi-purpose move – the bishop joins the attack, defends the c2 pawn, and vacates e2 for the white king.

5...♘d5

Black tries to coordinate his knight with his queen for the creation of counterplay, but disappointment awaits him.

6 ♖xd5! cxd5 7 fxg6 ♕c3+

7...♖b7 loses to 8 ♖h3!, e.g. 8...♕c3+ 9 ♔e2 e4 10 gxf7+ ♖xf7 11 ♖g3+, or 8...fxg6 9 ♕xg6+ ♔f8 10 ♕f6+ ♔g8 11 ♖g3+.

8 ♔e2 ♕c7

Black seems to have somehow managed to cover his weaknesses.

9 ♖h3!

The inclusion of the rook in the attack creates decisive threats against the black king.

9...fxg6 10 ♖g3 ♖h7

10...♖h6 also fails to save the game after 11 ♗xg6.

11 ♕xg6+ ♖g7 12 ♕h7+ Black resigns

Lempert–Tiviakov
St. Petersburg 1993

Black's extra pawn is scant consolation for the compromised position of his king, stuck in the centre. Even so, it is not easy for White to mount an attack, in view of his rather scattered pieces. In the search for harmony, it is tactics that come to his aid.

1 ♘c8+! ♔d8

Clearly, the knight sacrifice cannot be accepted – 1...♕xc8 2 ♕g7+.

2 ♕b1!

A brilliant swoop by the queen – tactics at the service of strategy!

Exploiting the fact that 2...♔xc8 is not possible on account of 3 ♖b8+!, mating, White coordinates his pieces. The knight at c8 is still immune, and its turn to participate in the attack will come.

2...e5

The white bishop is very dangerous, and it is quite logical that Black should aim to block it. Other continuations would also not have eased the defence, e.g. 2...♘h5 3 ♘a7! ♘xg3 4 ♘xc6+ dxc6 5 ♖b8+ ♔c7 6 ♖xf8 ♘e2+ 7 ♔h2 ♖xf8 8 ♕h7+, or 2...d6 3 ♘xd6 ♖xd6 4 ♗xd6 ♕xd6 5 ♖d1 ♘d5 6 c4.

3 ♗xe5!

By sacrificing his bishop, White fully activates all his remaining pieces.

3...♘xe5 4 ♖b8 ♘c6

4...♕g7 is even worse for Black in view of 5 ♘d6+ ♔e7 6 ♘f5+.

5 ♖e1!

White conducts the attack very resourcefully – the black king is under tight surveillance.

5...♘xb8 6 ♕xb8 ♘e4

A desperate attempt to create counterplay.

7 ♘d6+ ♔e7 8 ♖xe4+ ♔f6 9 ♘e8+

Of course, the more prosaic 9 ♖f4+ would also have won, but it is hard to refrain from giving a check with the knight that began the combination in this game.

9...♔g6

Here **Black lost on time**. But it is clear that after the forced 10 ♖xg4+

♔h5 11 ♕e5+! ♚xg4 12 ♘f6+ (or 12 f3+ immediately) 12...♕xf6 13 f3+! ♕xf3 14 gxf3+ ♚xf3 15 ♕xh8 he would all the same have had to concede defeat.

Chernin–Sznapik
Budapest 1993

A complicated, highly dynamic position. Black's kingside is weakened, and White's pieces are well coordinated for active play precisely on this part of the board. In completely seizing the initiative he is helped by a knight sacrifice.

1 ♖f3! gxf4

Otherwise White has a strong attack with material level.

2 ♖xf4 ♕e7

Comparatively best. The correctness of White's sacrifice is confirmed by the following variations: 2...♕e5 3 ♕g4+ ♚h8 (3...♕g7 4 ♕h4 h5 – or 4...♘g6 5 ♗xg6 – 5 ♕xh5 ♖e5 6 ♗f5) 4 ♖f5 ♕g7 5

♕h5 ♘g6 6 ♗xh6 ♕h7 7 ♖g5 ♘f4 8 ♗g7+, or 5...♖e5 6 ♗xh6 ♕h7 7 ♖xf8+ ♖xf8 8 ♗g7+, in both cases with decisive threats.

3 ♕h5!

This is stronger than 3 ♖g4+.

3...♗g7 4 ♖g4

White methodically strengthens the placing of his pieces, at the same time creating tactical threats.

4...♗c8

Black would also have lost quickly after 4...♕e5 5 ♗h7+! ♚xh7 6 ♖xe5 ♖xe5 7 ♕f7 ♖g5 8 ♗xg5 hxg5 9 ♖xg5.

5 ♖g3!

Emphasising the hopelessness of Black's position.

5...♕f7

Or 5...♚h8 6 ♗xh6 ♗xh6 7 ♕xh6+ ♘h7 8 ♗xh7 ♕xe1+ 9 ♔h2, and Black cannot save the game.

6 ♗h7+! ♘xh7 7 ♖xe8+ ♘f8 8 ♗c3!

The final finesse – the queen cannot be taken on account of mate. **Black resigns**.

Golubev–Verdihanov
Nikolaev 1993

Black is obviously behind in development, and his king is stuck in the centre.

White's pieces are very active, especially his queen and two knights, and it is this trio that begins to set the attack in motion. The first blow is struck by the knight at h4.

1 ♘g6! ♖g8

The immediate acceptance of the sacrifice is too naïve – 1...hxg6 2 fxg6 ♕e6 3 ♘xf6+ ♚d8 4 g7!, and White wins.

2 ♕h4! hxg6 3 fxg6!

White avoids the clever trap after 3 ♘xf6+ ♕xf6 4 ♕xf6 ♗e7, when he is obliged to return the queen.

3...♕e7

Or 3...♖xg6 4 ♘xf6+ ♖xf6 5 ♖xf6 ♕e7 6 ♕h5+, with decisive threats.

4 ♘xf6+ ♚d8 5 ♕h5! ♖g7 6 ♘d5

The queen/knight duo goes into action, splendidly assisted by the bishop and the rook at f1.

6...♕d6 7 ♕g5+ ♚e8

If 7...♗e7? 8 ♖f8 mate!

8 ♗xe5!

A splendid blow. It transpires that if 8...♕xd5 White wins by the simple 9 ♖xf8+! ♚xf8 10 ♗xg7+.

8...♘xe5 9 ♖xf8+!

The concluding stroke! Mate is inevitable, after both 9...♕xf8 10 ♘c7, and 9...♚xf8 10 ♕d8.

Black resigns

For the solving of each of the following tests (Nos. 9 to 12) the optimal time is 40-45 minutes.

TEST 9
Positions 56-61

56

So.Maus–Stangl
Germany 1993
Black to play

57

Glassner–Maahs
Germany 1993
White to play

58

Holzke–Lorincz
Budapest 1993
White to play

59

Gufeld–Tataev
Alushta 1993
White to play

60
Hodgson–Crouch
Dublin (Zonal) 1993
Black to play

61
Makarov–Tringov
Arandelovac 1993
White to play

TEST 10
Positions 62-67

62
Kurajica–Soloviov
San Sebastian 1993
White to play

63
Krasenkov–Dvoiris
Rostov 1993
White to play

64
Ubilava–Huguet
Ibercaja 1993
White to play

65
Vyzhmanavin–Voiska
Ibercaja 1993
White to play

66
Izeta–Antunes
Benasque 1993
Black to play

67
Bakh–Vajda
Odorheiu 1993
Black to play

TEST 11
Positions 68-73

68
Mitkov–Bernard
Paris 1993
White to play

69
Birk–Gabriel
Germany 1993
White to play

70
Zude–Del Rio
Germany 1993
White to play

71
Naumkin–Arkell
London (Lloyds Bank) 1993
White to play

72
Shabalov–Smyslov
Tilburg 1993
White to play

73
Vukic–Gavric
Serbia 1993
Black to play

TEST 12
Positions 74-79

74
Yakovich–Steinbacher
Ostend 1993
White to play

75
Kir.Georgiev–Adams
Groningen 1993
Black to play

76
Wirthensohn–Forster
Switzerland 1993
White to play

77
Kumaran–Miles
Dublin (Zonal) 1993
White to play

78
Cvitan–Rogic
Zagreb 1993
White to play

79
Kaminski–Davies
Liechtenstein 1993
Black to play

6   The Pawn

Pawns take a very active part in many attacks and combinations. Right from the opening the pawn structure determines how the play develops on this or that part of the board.

A flexible and mobile pawn chain can have a marked influence on the dynamics of the resulting positions. Classic pawn attacks in the centre and on the flanks have become text-book examples. The sacrifice of a pawn for the initiative is the stimulus of many combinational ideas, and has become one of the most approved procedures in modern chess.

In this chapter we will examine examples of combinational play by pawns in all stages of the game. Usually a combinational blow by a pawn is the prelude to the start of a combination or attack, but sometimes tactical play with pawns is of an independent nature. The value of a pawn grows particularly in combinations, carried out in order to promote it to a queen.

Rakic–Popcev
Novi Sad 1993

White has two pawns for a piece, but the value of one of them, at f7, is very high. His knight at e6 is also active. It is this knight and the pawns that will play the leading role in the coming combination.

Black's threat of ...axb3+ is unpleasant, but he does not manage to create real counterplay.

1 dxc5!! axb3+

If 1...dxc5 White would simply have played 2 ♘xc5+ followed by ♘xa4, and then set in motion his avalanche of pawns on the queenside.

2 axb3!

The less spectacular 2 ♔xb3 is also less clear.

2...♖xa1 3 ♖xa1 ♖xa1 4 g5!

White's knight and pawns battle successfully against the opponent's superior forces.

4...♗g7 5 ♘xg7 ♖f1

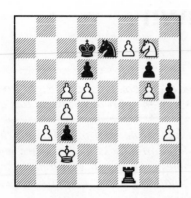

6 c6+! ♘xc6
Forced: 6...♔c8 is met by 7 ♘e8!
7 dxc6+ ♔c8
Everything else also loses quickly:
7...♔xc6 8 ♘e6 ♖xf7 9 ♘d8+, or
7...♔c7 8 f8=♕ ♖xf8 9 ♘e6+.
8 ♘e8 ♔d8 9 c7+
9 ♘f6 would also have won.
9...♔c8 10 ♘f6 Black resigns

Topalov–Adams
Las Palmas 1993

Black appears to have been more successful in his attack – the concentration of his pieces on the kingside is very considerable. But it is White's turn to move, and he begins a spectacular combination, weaving a mating net around the opponent's king. The resulting pawn trio on the queenside plays the leading role in the attack.

1 ♘c5+! ♘xc5 2 dxc5
Threatening 3 c6+.
2...♔b8 3 ♕xf6
The picture has changed sharply – the white pieces have become active, successfully combining attack with the defence of their king.
**3...♖f5 4 ♕d4 ♗xe2 5 ♖e1 hxg3
6 ♖xg3! ♖xg3+ 7 fxg3**
If 7 hxg3 Black has the unpleasant 7...h2+!
7...♕e8
Black covers his weak back rank and defends his bishop, but this results in his queen being overloaded. If 7...♕f7 White wins by 8 ♕h8+ ♔b7 9 c6+ ♔b6 10 ♕d4+.

8 Xe2! Black resigns

Since after 8...♕xe2 9 ♕h8+ ♔b7 10 c6+ ♔b6 11 ♕d4+ ♔a5 12 ♗d2+ he has to give up his queen.

Nevednichy–Ionescu
Bucharest 1993

For an attack on the black king, White must activate his light-square bishop. In order to break up the king's pawn screen, the sacrifices at f6 and h7 suggest themselves. White implements this idea in spectacular fashion.

1 e5!

Signalling the start of the attack.

1...dxe5

If the knight moves, then 2 ♗xh7+ wins.

2 Xxf6! gxf6

Better than 2...exd4?, when White wins by force: 3 ♗xh7+ ♔h8 4 ♕h5 gxf6 5 ♗f5+ ♔g8 6 ♕xe8+ ♔g7 7 ♗h6+! ♔xh6 8 ♕g6 mate. And after 2...♗xf6 3 ♗xh7+ ♔f8 4 ♘f3 he retains a dangerous attack.

3 ♘xe6!

Much stronger than 3 ♕h5 exd4 4 ♕xe8+ ♔g7 5 ♗xd4 ♕c6!, with counterplay for Black.

3...♕f7

White's attack would have developed in interesting fashion after 3...Xxe6, e.g. 4 ♕g4+ ♔f7 5 ♘d5 ♕d7 6 ♗xh7 ♗xd5 7 cxd5 Xe8 8 ♗f5 ♕xd5 9 ♗e4 ♕xa2 10 ♗xa8.

Here 5 ♗xh7 is also quite possible, with dangerous threats.

4 ♘xd8 Xxd8 5 ♗xb6

For the exchange White has a pawn and an obvious positional advantage.

J.Polgar–Ftacnik
Budapest 1993

It might be assumed that, with a spatial advantage in the centre and on the kingside, it is here that White will try to create pressure. On the c-file, the only one open, a mass exchange of the heavy pieces may take place.

But White embarks on a pawn offensive on the queenside, opening up the position here, hoping thereby to exploit the weakness of the dark squares to mount an attack against the opponent's king.

1 a4! bxa4

Black accepts the challenge. No better was 1...e5 2 ♘b3 bxa4 3 ♘a5 followed by ♘d5.

2 b5! axb5

White gains a pretty piece attack in the event of 2...♗b7 3 ♘xa4 ♖xc1+ 4 ♖xc1 axb5 5 ♘b6 ♕d8 6 ♘xe6! fxe6 7 ♘d7!, or 2...e5 3 bxa6! exd4 4 ♕b2+ ♗b7 5 ♗xd4.

3 ♘dxb5 a3

For the moment it is only the two sides' pawns that are in the action. Black is unable to gain counterplay – 3...♕b7 4 ♕b2 a3 5 ♕b3 ♖c6 6 ♗a7+ ♔c8 7 ♗d4.

4 ♘xa3 ♖c7 5 ♕b2+! ♖b7 6 ♘cb5 ♖f8

A very complicated, double-edged position, where the insecure

placing of both kings creates the preconditions for tactical blows. Even so, White's pieces are more active and better coordinated.

7 ♗a7+!

By sacrificing two minor pieces for a rook, White not only draws the black king out of his shelter, but also eliminates the threats to her own king.

7...♖xa7 8 ♘xa7+ ♔xa7 9 ♘b5+ ♔b8

Forced: if 9...♔a6 White wins by 10 ♕a2+! ♔b6 (or 10...♔xb5 11 ♖e2) 11 ♘d4! ♘c7 12 ♖e2, when the black king succumbs to the direct attack by the opponent's heavy pieces.

10 ♘d4+

10 ♘xd6+ ♗b7 11 ♖c8+ ♕xc8 12 ♘xc8 ♔xc8 is not so clear.

10...♗b7 11 ♘c6+ ♔c8 12 ♘e5+ ♕c7 13 ♖xc7+ ♘xc7 14 ♘c4

White has not only a decisive material advantage, but also a positional one. Through inertia Black made a few more moves, but soon resigned.

Vlassov–Martin
Passau 1993

The position is an open one, and this is clearly to the advantage of the more active white pieces. It is interesting to see how the coordination of the black pieces is totally destroyed by two tactical pawn blows.

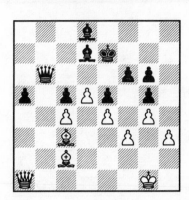

1 g4! ♕xg4

Black's queen needs to keep his bishop defended – on 1...♕f3 White would have won by 2 ♖xd7! ♔xd7 3 ♗xb5+.

2 e6!

Forcing a spectacular win. If now 2...♗xe6, then 3 ♗xb5+ ♔f8 4 ♕xa5!

2...fxe6 3 ♖xd7!

This exchange sacrifice has been constantly in the air.

3...♔xd7 4 ♗xb5+ ♘c6 5 ♗e5!

Now it is clear what position White had in mind when he began the combination, and why he required the move 1 g4!

5...♖ac8

5...♖hc8 would also have lost after 6 ♕d6+ ♔e8 7 ♗xc6+ ♔f7 8 ♗xa8 ♖c1+ 9 ♔d2 ♖xh1 10 ♕d7+, while if 5...♖hd8 6 ♕d6+ ♔e8 7 ♕xc6+ and 8 ♗e2 with a winning position.

6 ♕d6+ ♔e8 7 ♗xc6+ ♖xc6 8 ♕xc6+ ♔f7 9 ♕d7+

Black resigns

White's pieces are the more active, and his protected passed d-pawn is clearly stronger than the black pawn at a5. But for the moment the blocked pawn chains prevent White from making use of his pluses. He needs to open up the position.

1 h4!!

A fine thematic pawn sacrifice, which Black is forced to accept.

1...gxh4 2 g5!

A further, temporary pawn sacrifice, since Black cannot allow the opponent a pair of connected passed pawns after 2...fxg5? 3 ♗xe5.

2...♗c7 3 f4!

The pawn onslaught continues. It is unfavourable for Black himself to relieve the tension – 3...fxg5 4 fxe5 or 3...exf4 4 gxf6+, while 3...♕d6 is strongly met by 4 ♕e1!

3...♕b8 4 gxf6+ ♔xf6 5 ♕f1! ♔g7 6 fxe5 ♗xe5 7 ♕f4! Black resigns

Kramnik–Serper
Dortmund 1993

It is risky for White to open up the centre, since Black's dark-square bishop is active, and on the queen-side too there are no prospects. White's plan is a pawn offensive on the kingside, and within a few moves the picture changes radically.

1 g4! ♘f8

Black covers the weaknesses at g6 and h7, and includes his queen in the defence of the kingside.

2 g5!

Much stronger than 2 h4 g6 3 g5 ♗g7, when White's attack is not so effective.

2...hxg5 3 fxg5 ♗e7 4 e4!

All White's pieces are active in the centre, and are ready to participate in the attack on the opponent's king.

4...dxe4 5 ♕xe4 ♖ad8 6 ♖e2

6 ♕g4 was also pretty strong.

6...a6 7 ♕g4 ♕a5 8 ♘e5!

Black resigns, since he has no way of opposing the direct attack on

the king. 8...♖xd4 is met by 9 ♕h5 g6 10 ♖xf8+!

Uhlmann–Wahls
Erfurt 1993

Resolute action is required of White, otherwise Black's counter-play on the queenside will become very dangerous. A classical rule goes into operation – against a flank attack, answer with a blow (or attack) in the centre.

1 e5!

Blocking the bishop at g7 and not fearing 1...bxc4 in view of 2 ♗e4 dxe5 3 f5! ♖b8 4 fxg6 f5 5 ♖xh3 and then ♗xf5. White's entire strategic concept is based on precise calculation.

1...dxe5 2 f5!

A typical example of a pawn attack. After the opening of the game, the scattered nature of Black's pieces tells.

2...♘b6

2...bxc4 is again bad on account of 3 fxg6! f5 4 ♖xh3! cxd3 5 ♖xh8+ ♚xh8 6 ♕g2!, with a decisive attack.

3 d6!

Now 3 fxg6 f5 4 ♖xh3 ♖xh3 5 ♗xf5 ♘xc4 is ineffective.

3...exd6

White's tactical idea was 3...bxc4 4 fxg6! f5 5 ♗xc4+! ♘xc4 6 ♕d5+. The d-pawn has played an important role.

4 f6!

White's pawn attack is an excellent textbook example.

4...♗xf6 5 ♗xg6!

Beginning a direct piece attack on the king.

5...♖d8

If 5...♘xc4 White wins with the simple 6 ♗d3+, followed by ♗xc4 and ♕xd6.

6 ♕f2! ♘d7 7 ♗f5+ ♚f8 8 ♗xd7 Black resigns

Karpov–Kasparov
Linares 1993

White has played the opening badly, and his pieces are passive and are eeking out a pitiful existence. He has some hopes of play with his heavy pieces on the h-file, but this is scant consolation for the compromised position of his king.

To gain a decisive advantage, Black needs to activate his pieces still further.

1...c4!

It is now clear that 2 bxc4 is bad on account of 2...♕a5!, when the combined attack on the white king is decisive. But what can be done with the irrepressible c-pawn?

2 ♘c1 c3!!

A picturesque position! The white pieces are so passive, that Black can permit himself this sacrifice. White has no choice.

3 ♘xa2 c2 4 ♕d4

The only move, since Black would have won very prettily after 4 ♖c1 ♘xe5! 5 ♖xc2 ♗g4 6 ♖d2 ♘xd2 7 ♘xd2 ♖e8 8 fxe5 ♖xe5+ 9

&f2 ♕xd2+ 10 &g3 ♖e3+ 11 &h2
♖h3! mate.

4...cxd1=♕+ 5 &xd1

5 ♕xd1 is no better in view of
5...♘g3 6 ♖h3 ♘xf1 7 &xf1 ♘c5 8
♕xd8 ♖xd8 9 ♖e3 ♖d1+ 10 ♖e1
♗a6+ 11 &f2 ♘d3+, when Black
wins.

5...♘dc5!

Even the exchange of queens does
not save White – the black pieces
are too active.

6 ♕xd8 ♖xd8+ 7 &c2

No better was 7 &e1 ♗g4, or 7
&c1 ♘f2 followed by ...♖d1+.

7...♘f2

White resigns, without waiting
for the mate after 8 ♖g1 ♗f5+ 9
&b2 ♘d1+ 10 &a1 (10 &c1 ♘xb3
mate!) 10...♘xb3.

A.Rodriguez–Sorin
Matanzas 1993

White's pieces are the more
active, and the black king is still in
the centre. Black's bishop at g4 and
knight at g6 are lending stability to
his position on the kingside. White
needs to cause disharmony among
the black pieces and to further
activate his own. An appropriate
moment for a pawn attack.

1 e6! ♗xe6 2 h4!

Just two pawn moves have been
made, but what a striking change on
the board! Black cannot prevent
h4-h5, and he cannot castle in view
of 2...0-0 3 h5 ♘e7 4 ♗h6 g6 5
♕e5! All that remains is the move
in the game, but it too does not save
him from an attack.

**2...&d7!? 3 h5 ♘e7 4 ♕xg7 ♖g8
5 ♕f6!**

Black is practically in *zugzwang*.

**5...♕e8 6 ♗g5 h6!? 7 ♗xh6 ♖g4
8 ♗f4!**

Setting up an attack on the dark
squares and making way for the
h-pawn.

**8...♖g8 9 g3 ♕a8 10 ♕e5 ♕a5
11 h6**

Black resigns

The optimal time to solve the following test is 55-60 minutes.

80
Suba–Sax
Budapest (Zonal) 1993
Black to play

81
Wojtkiewicz–Rasik
Budapest (Zonal) 1993
White to play

82
Meyers–Djurhuus
Biel 1993
White to play

83
Akopian–S.Ivanov
St Petersburg 1993
White to play

84
Shirov–Lobron
Munich 1993
White to play

85
P.Perez – Cruz-Lima
Cuba 1993
Black to play

86
Kaminski–Stefansson
Capelle la Grande 1993
Black to play

87
Taborov–Vovk
Kiev 1993
White to play

88
Barua-Nikolic
Biel (Zonal) 1993
White to play

89
S.Guliev–Tukmakov
Nikolaev (Zonal) 1993
White to play

7 Various Combinations

The combinations given in this book certainly do not exhaust the entire tactical diversity in games from 1993. It quite often happens that a combinational fragment does not reach a logical conclusion, on account of inaccuracies and mistakes by the players, distorting the logical outcome of the game. It can also happen that attack and defence cancel each other out, and the game ends in a draw.

Such games and fragments also provide a certain interest. Here we will only dwell on a few, the most striking examples.

Timman–Murrey
France 1993

---

1 e4 e5 2 ♘f3 ♘f6 3 d4 ♘xe4 4 ♗d3

In this well-studied position, instead of the usual 4...d5 Black unexpectedly played

4...♘c6!?

This piece sacrifice is a temporary one – 5 ♗xe4 d5 and then ...e5-e4, but nevertheless very spectacular.

5 ♗xe4

If 5 d5 Black has the satisfactory reply 5...♘c5! 6 ♗e2 e4!

5...d5 6 ♗g5 ♕d7

After 6...f6 7 ♘xe5! ♘xe5 8 dxe5 dxe4 9 ♕xd8+ ♔xd8 10 exf6 White gains an obvious advantage.

6...♕d6 was interesting, with the threat of ...♕b4+.

7 ♗d3! e4 8 0-0 f6 9 ♖e1! ♗e7 10 ♗f4 exd3 11 ♕xd3 0-0

Black's position is slightly inferior, but quite sound.

Brinck-Claussen – Sher
Farum 1993

White's pawn offensive on the kingside is somewhat delayed, whereas Black has been quite successful in creating counterplay on the queenside.

Whose king is in the greater danger? With a far from obvious and highly spectacular combination,

White emphasizes his advantage and retains the initiative.

1 ♗xh7+! ♔xh7 2 ♘f5! exf5

Black is forced to accept White's sacrifices; 3 exd6 was threatened.

3 ♘d5 ♕c6

On 3...♕d7 or 3...♕d8 White would have won most simply by 4 ♗xc5. The queen at c6 retains hopes of counterplay.

4 ♕h5+ ♔g8

The critical position. The logical completion of White's splendid combination was 5 ♗xc5, e.g. 5...♕xc5 6 ♘f6+! ♗xf6 7 gxf6, or 5...dxc5 6 ♘f6+! ♗xf6 7 gxf6 followed by ♖hg1.

This exchange on c5 would have deprived Black of any chances of counterplay. But White, carried away by his attack, overestimates his threats.

5 ♘f6+?! ♗xf6

Of course, not 5...gxf6 6 gxf6, when the black king succumbs.

6 gxf6 dxe5 7 fxe5?

One inaccuracy gives rise to another. 7 fxg7 was stronger, in the hope of 7...♔xg7 8 ♖hg1+ ♔f8 9 ♕h6+! ♕xh6 10 ♗xc5+ ♕d6 11 ♗xd6+ ♖e7 12 h5 ♘b7 13 h6!, but Black can play more strongly – 7...♘d3+! 8 ♔b1 f6! 9 ♖hg1 ♗e6, when the outcome of White's attack is problematic.

7...♘d3+! 8 ♔b1

It is possible that initially White had been planning 8 ♖xd3 ♕xh1+ 9 ♖d1, but then he noticed that after 9...♕e4, with the threats of ...♕xe3+ or ...♕g4, Black would have repulsed the straightforward attack.

8...♘xe5 9 fxg7 f6 10 ♖hg1 ♘f7

A dismal outcome for such a spectacular combination. White soon resigned the game.

Agdestein–Lendwai
Cappelle la Grande 1993

The game has essentially not yet gone out of the opening. At first sight Black appears to have insufficient grounds for creating tactical threats. The only pretext is the white king at e1 and the vulnerable f2 pawn. But this alone, in combination with the the storming advance of the active pawns in the centre, is sufficient to start a combination.

1...♘xf2!
A blow at the "Achilles' heel".
2 ♔xf2 e4 3 ♖d1!
A sensible decision – White returns the piece, otherwise Black would have gained a direct attack on the king, e.g. 3 ♘g1 f4! 4 exf4 e3+! 5 ♗xe3 ♖xe3! 6 ♔xe3 ♗c5+.
3...exf3 4 gxf3 f4! 5 exf4 ♘d4! 6 ♕d3 c5 7 h4 b6
After the tactical complications Black is a pawn down, but he has more than sufficient compensation for it. White's king is insecure, and his kingside pawns are weakened, and the black pieces are ready to take the initiative.

Unfortunately, in the subsequent play Black made a number of errors, and White succeeded in stabilising

the position and then seizing the initiative – what told was his higher standard of play.

Van Wely–Kramnik
Biel 1993

This is a position from the Botvinnik Variation of the Slav Defence, which is noted for its especially sharp and dynamic play. Black has been unable to castle and his queenside pawns, especially the one at c4, are weak. But here he makes a paradoxical move, based on tactical calculation.
1...♖h4!?
It is fortunate for White that in chess one is not obliged to capture, since after 2 gxh4 ♖g8 Black would have gained a very strong attack.
2 ♕d2!
With the threat of ♕g5+.
2...♖d4
This unusual rook manoeuvre is insufficient to cement together Black's position, and White is the

first to approach the opponent's king. Kramnik had another extravagent possibility – 2...♘f4!?

But here too White would have parried all the threats and gained a decisive advantage after 3 ♘xc4 ♛c7 4 f3 ♘xg2 5 ♛g5+ ♚f8 6 gxh4 ♘f4 7 ♚h1.

3 ♛g5+ ♘f6 4 ♗xb7 ♖g8

4...♛xb7? 5 ♛xc5+ with an easy win.

5 ♛e5 ♘d7 6 ♛e2 ♛xb7 7 ♘xc4

If it is assumed that Kramnik had planned 1...♖h4!? during his preparations for the game, then the evaluation of this position, which is reached almost by force, must have been clear to him – White has the advantage. Evidently Black was very much relying on the psychological effect of the unusual rook move, and he thereby overstepped the limit of acceptable risk.

(see diagram next column)

7...♖h4

Returning the rook to its initial position, Black sets the transparent threat of 8...♖xh2. But all in vain...

8 f3 ♛c7 9 ♘e3! ♚f8 10 ♘g4 ♖h5 11 ♖ad1

White has stablised the position and gained a technically won ending, which after a stubborn resistance Black eventually resigned.

Christiansen–Anand
Las Palmas 1993

Black has won the h2 pawn, but in doing so he has fallen behind in development. The position of his king at e8 and queen at c7 create the preconditions for a combined attack; the knight sacrifice at b5 suggests itself.

1 ♘cxb5! ♕e7

If 1...axb5 White wins by 2 ♕xb5+, while 1...♕b6 2 ♖xc5 could have transposed into the game.

2 ♖xc5!?

A tempting exchange sacrifice – White is aiming at all costs for an attack on the king. However, he did not have any real choice – 2 ♘c3 could have been met by 2...f5!?, when unexpectedly there are threats to the white king.

2...♕xc5 3 ♘xe6!

The main idea of White's combination is revealed in the variation 3...♕xb5 4 ♕h5!, with the threats of ♘c7+ or ♘g7+ and a deadly blow by the queen at f7.

3...fxe6 4 ♕h5+ ♔e7

(*see diagram next column*)

5 ♗xe6!

Another spectacular blow, by which White guarantees himself a draw.

5...♔xe6

If 5...♖hf8 White wins by 6 ♖d7+ (or 6 ♕xh7+ ♔xe6 7 ♕d7 mate) 6...♔xe6 7 ♕f5 mate.

6 ♕g4+ ♔f7 7 ♖d7+ ♕e7 8 ♕h5+ ♔f8 9 ♕h6+ ♔f7 10 ♖xe7+ ♔xe7 11 ♕g7+

Unfortunately for White, his queen and knight are unable to achieve the coordination required to continue the attack.

11...♔e6 12 ♕g4+ ♔e7 13 ♕g7+ ♔e6 14 ♕xb7

In any event the game ends in perpetual check.

14...axb5 15 ♕d5+ ♔e7 16 ♕b7+ ♔e6 17 ♕d5+

Draw agreed

For the solving of the final test, 40-45 minutes are allowed.

TEST 14
Positions 90-96

90

Shirov–Kramnik
Groningen 1993
Black to play

91

Kasparov–Short
London 1993 (7th match game)
White to play

92

Atalik–Miles
Iraklion 1993
Black to play

93

De La Paz–Pujols
Cuba 1993
White to play

94
Cruz-Lima – Hernandez
Cuba 1993
White to play

95
Kuznetsov–Kotkov
Russia 1993
White to play

96
Bayona–Aristizabal
Columbia 1993
Black to play

Solutions to the Tests

1. 1 ♕xa2! (1 ♕xe6+ ♔h7 2 ♕f5+ ♔g8 3 ♖c2 also wins) 1...♘xa2 2 ♖c8+ ♔h7 3 ♖h8+! ♔xh8 4 ♘g6+ and wins.

2. 1 ♕xh6+! gxh6 2 ♘f7+ ♔g8 3 ♘xh6 mate.

3. 1...♕d2+! 2 ♗xd2 f2 mate.

4. 1 ♕xg7+! ♔xg7 2 ♖d7+ ♔h8 3 ♗h6 ♘e8 (3...♖g8 4 hxg8=♕+ ♔xg8 5 ♘e4 ♘d5 6 ♖xd5 ♖f8 7 ♖d7 ♕b6 8 ♖g7+ ♔h8 9 ♖h7+ ♔g8 10 ♖h8+!) 4 ♖f7 Black resigns.

5. 1...♕xf5! 2 ♗xf5 (2 ♖xe2 ♖xh2+ 3 ♖xh2 ♕f1 mate) 2...♖xh2+ White resigns (3 ♔g1 ♗d4 mate).

6. 1...♕xg2+! White resigns (2 ♔xg2 ♗e4+ 3 ♔g1 ♘h3 mate).

7. 1 ♕d6! Black resigns (1...gxh5 2 ♕xe5 f6 3 ♕g3+).

8. 1 ♕xh7+! (in fact there is also a forced mate by 1 ♖xf7+ ♔xf7 2 ♕xh7+ ♔f6 3 ♖f8+ ♔g5 4 h4) 1...♔xh7 2 ♖xf7+ ♔h6 3 ♖h8+ Black resigns (3...♔g5 4 h4 mate).

9. 1 ♕xg6!! Black resigns (1...hxg6 2 ♖h4).

10. 1 ♖xe7! ♘xe7 (1...♗xe7 2 ♗xd5+ ♔b6 3 ♘xh8 ♗b7 4 ♗xb7 ♔xb7 5 ♖d7+ ♔b6 6 ♖xe7 fxg2 7 ♖e1 and wins) 2 ♘d8+ ♔b6 3 ♖d6+ ♔c7 (3...♔a5 4 ♗d2+ ♔a4 5 ♗b3+ ♔b5 6 a4 mate) 4 ♖d3+! Black resigns (4...♔b6 5 ♖b3+ ♔a5 6 ♗c7+ ♔a4 7 ♗b5 mate).

11. 1...♖e2!! 2 ♕xe2 ♖xb3+! 3 ♔c1 (3 axb3 ♕a1+ 4 ♔c2 ♕b2+ 5 ♔d3 ♕c3 mate) 3...♕c3+ White resigns (4 ♔c2 ♖b1+! 5 ♔xb1 ♕a1 mate).

12. 1...♖xe3! 2 fxe3 ♖xe3 3 ♔g2 ♕xf4 4 ♖f1 (or 4 ♖e1 ♖d3!) 4...♕e4+ 5 ♔g1 cxb3 6 ♖xc7 ♖e2 7 ♖f2 ♕g4+ White resigns.

13. 1 ♖xh7!! ♗xh7 2 ♕h5? (2 g6! ♗xg6 3 ♕h1 is correct, when White wins) 2...♗c5 3 ♗f6 ♗xc2+?? (Black could have won by 3...♕e1+ 4 ♔b2 ♕d2!, e.g. 5 g6 ♗d4+ 6 ♗xd4 ♕xd4+) 4 ♔xc2 Black resigns.

14. 1 ♖xd5! cxd5 2 ♕c7+ ♔g8 3 ♕d8+ ♔g7 4 ♕d7+ ♔h8 (4...♔h6 5 ♘f7+ ♔g7 6 ♘g5+) 5 ♘f7+ ♔g8 6 ♘h6+ ♔h8 7 ♕d8+ Black resigns (7...♔g7 8 ♕g8+ ♔xh6 9 ♕h8 mate).

15. 1 ♖h8+! ♔f7 2 ♕e3!! ♕f5 (2...exf3+ 3 gxf3 and wins) 3 ♖ch1! exf3+ 4 gxf3 ♕e5 5 ♖1h7+ ♔f6 6 ♖f8+ ♔g5 7 ♖xf4 ♕xf4 8 ♕e7+ Black resigns.

16. 1 ♖xh4 gxh4 2 ♗e3 ♘xc6 3 ♕xc6 ♕a8 4 ♕d7+ ♖e7 5 ♕f5 Black resigns.

17. 1 ♖e7+! (1 ♖xf5 gxf5 2 ♖e7+ ♔h6 3 h3 also wins, although less attractively) 1...♔h6 2 ♕g7+! ♘xg7 3 ♗xg7+ ♔h7 4 ♗xf8+ ♔g8 5 ♖dxd7+ ♔xf8 6 ♖f7+ Black resigns.

TEST 3
Positions 18-23

18. 1...♖h1+! White resigns (2 ♔xh1 ♖h8+ 3 ♔g1 ♖h1+! 4 ♔xh1 ♕h8+ 5 ♔g1 ♕h2 mate).

19. 1 ♖xh7! ♘xh7 2 ♕e6+ ♔h8 3 ♖h1 ♘df6 4 ♖xh7+! Black resigns (4...♘xh7 5 ♕h3).

20. 1 ♖xe6!! fxe6 2 f7 ♕f8 3 ♘xe6 ♕h6 4 ♘f8+ ♔e7 5 ♘g6+ ♔xf7 6 ♕d7+ ♔g8 7 ♕e6+ Black resigns

21. 1...♖xf2!! 2 ♔xf2 ♗xd4+ 3 ♔f3 ♗g4+! White resigns.

22. 1 ♖xh7! ♔xh7 2 ♕h5+ ♔g8 3 ♗xg6 ♖fb8 4 ♗h7+ (4 ♗f7+ ♔f8 5 ♗e6 wins more quickly) 4...♔f8 5 e6 ♗e8 6 ♕f5+ ♗f6 7 ♕g4 ♗g7 8 0-0-0 ♗f7 9 exf7 ♔xf7 10 ♕g6+ Black resigns.

23. 1 g4+!! ♔xe4 2 ♘f2+ ♔xf4 3 ♖g1! Black resigns (3...e4 4 ♘h3 mate).

TEST 4
Positions 24-30

24. 1 ♖xd3! ♖xd3 2 b4! ♖d5+ 3 ♔c6 ♖d6+ 4 ♔c5 ♖d8 5 bxa5 e4 6 fxe4 fxe4 7 a6 e3 8 a7 e2 9 b8=♕ Draw agreed.

25. 1 ♖xd5! gxh5 2 ♖xf5! ♘f8 3 ♖xh5 bxa2 4 ♗xa2 ♗g7 5 ♕g4 ♔h8 6 ♗xg7+ ♕xg7 7 ♖g5 ♘g6 8 ♗b1 ♕c3 9 ♖d1 ♕f6 10 ♖d7 ♖e7 11 ♖xe7 ♕xe7 12 ♗xg6 ♖g8 13 ♕d4+ ♖g7 14 ♖h5 e5 Black resigns.

26. 1 ♖g7+! ♔xg7 2 ♕f6+ ♔g8 3 ♕f8+ ♔h7 4 ♕f7+ ♔h6 5 ♗f8+ ♔g5 (5...♔h5 6 ♕h7+ ♔g4 7 ♕h3+ ♔g5 8 ♗e7+ ♔f4 9 ♕g3+ ♔f5 10 ♕g5+ mate) 6 h4+ ♔xh4 7 ♕h7+ ♔g5 8 ♗e7+ ♔f4 (8...♔f5 9 ♕h3+ ♕g4 10 ♕d3+ ♕e4 11 g4+ and wins) 9 ♕h4+ Black resigns.

27. 1 ♖xe6! fxe6 (or 1...♗xf3 2 gxf3 fxe6 3 ♕xg6+ ♗g7 4 ♕h7+ ♔f7 5 ♗g6+ ♔f6 6 ♗h5, when 6...♖h8 is strongly met by 7 ♖e1) 2 ♕xg6+ ♗g7 3 ♕h7+ ♔f7 4 ♗g6+ ♔f6 5 ♗h5 ♖h8 (5...d5 6 ♕g6+ ♔e7 7 ♕xg7+ ♔d6 8 ♕xb7 and wins) 6 ♕xh6+ ♔e7 7 ♕h7+ ♔f6 8 ♕xb7 ♕e7 9 ♕e4 Black resigns.

28. 1 ♖xf7+! ♖xf7 2 ♕xh6+! ♔g8 3 ♕h8+! ♔xh8 4 ♘xf7+ Black resigns.

29. 1 ♖h8+! ♗xh8 2 ♕xg5+ ♗g7 3 ♘f6+ ♔f8 4 ♖h8+! Black resigns (4...♗xh8 5 ♘h7 mate).

30. 1 ♖e8+! Black resigns (1...♔xe8 2 ♘f6+ ♔f8 3 ♘d7+, or 2...♔e7 3 ♖e1+ ♔f8 4 ♘d7+).

TEST 5
Positions 31-37

31. 1 ♕h6! ♕xc3 (1...♗xf6 2 ♕xf6 0-0 3 ♗d3 and wins) 2 ♖xe6+! fxe6 3 ♕xe6+ ♔d8 4 ♗g4 ♖a7 5 ♕xd5+ ♔e8 6 ♗h5+ ♔f8 7 ♕d8+ Black resigns.

32. 1 ♖xg7+! ♕xg7 2 ♖g1 ♘hf6 3 ♗h6 Black resigns.

33. 1 ♖xc4! ♕xc4 2 ♖d8+! ♔f7 3 ♕h5+ g6 (3...♔e6 4 ♖xc8) 4 ♕xh7+ Black resigns (4...♔e6 5 ♕g8+).

34. 1 ♖xb7! ♘xb7 (1...♖xb7 2 ♘xc5 ♕xc5 3 ♕e4 and wins) 2 ♘f6+! gxf6 3 ♕g4+ ♔h8 4 ♕h4 f5 5 ♕f6+ ♔g8 6 ♗h6 ♗e5 7 ♕xf5 Black resigns.

35. 1 ♖xd5 exd5 2 ♕xd5+ ♔h8 3 ♖xh6+! gxh6 4 ♕f7 Black resigns.

36. 1...♖xf2! 2 ♔xf2 ♖c2+ 3 ♔e3 ♕c3+! 4 ♔xe4 ♖e2+ 5 ♔d5 ♖d2+ 6 ♔e4 ♕d3+ White resigns.

37. 1...♖xd3! 2 ♖xd3 ♗xg2+! 3 ♕xg2 ♕b1+ 4 ♔h2 Draw agreed.

TEST 6
Positions 38-43

38. 1 ♖hf1! axb3 2 ♖xf6! ♘a3+ 3 ♔c1 b2+ 4 ♔d2 ♕xc3+ 5 ♔e2 ♗g4+ 6 ♔f2 Black resigns.

39. 1 ♗xd5! ♔d8 2 ♕d1! ♗xf5 3 ♗xc6+ ♔c7 4 ♗d7+ ♔b6 5 ♕b3+ Black resigns.

40. 1...♗xh3! 2 ♖ae1 (2 gxh3 ♖xh3 3 ♘e4 ♕f3 4 ♘g3 ♖xg3+) 2...♗xg2! 3 ♖e7 (3 ♔xg2 ♕f3+ 4 ♔g1 – or 4 ♔f1 ♖d2 – 4...♕g4+ 5 ♔f1 ♖h3 or 5...♖g3) 3...♕h5 4 ♔xg2 ♕g4+ 5 ♔f1 ♖g3 White resigns.

41. 1 ♗xf7+! ♖xf7 2 ♖e8+ ♗f8 3 ♘e5 ♕f6 4 ♘e4 ♕f4 5 ♖xc6 (5 ♖xf8+! ♔xf8 6 ♘xg6+) 5...♔g7 6 g3 ♕f5 7 g4 ♕f4 8 ♖xg6+ ♔h7 9 ♘g5+! Black resigns.

42. 1...♗g5!! 2 fxg4 (2 ♗xg5 ♕a1+ 3 ♗f1 ♗c4, 2 ♕e1 ♗xd2 3 ♕xd2 ♕a1+ 4 ♗f1 ♗c4, or 2 ♔e1 ♗f4 3 ♕h4 g5 intending ...♕a1, and in each case Black wins) 2...♗xd2 3 ♔f1 ♗xg4! White resigns.

43. 1 ♗xg7! (White also has a simple win by 1 ♕e5 f6 2 ♕d5+) 1...♕c5+ (1...♔xg7 2 ♕xh6+ ♔g8 3 ♕g5+ intending ♖h6) 2 ♗d4 ♕g5 3 ♖xh6! Black resigns.

TEST 7
Positions 44-49

---

44. 1 ♘d7! ♖xb5 2 ♘xf6+ ♔g7 3 ♕xh7+ ♔xf6 4 ♕h8+ ♔g5 5 h4+ Black resigns.

45. 1 ♗xg6! ♘f4 (1...fxg6 2 ♕e6+ ♔f8 3 ♗xg7+ ♔xg7 4 ♕xg6+) 2 ♗xf7+ ♔xf7 3 ♖xg7+ ♔f8 4 ♕e4 e5 5 ♕f5+! ♔xg7 6 ♖g1+ Black resigns (6...♔h6 7 ♕g5+ ♔h7 8 ♕h4+).

46. 1 ♗xh7+! ♔xh7 2 ♕h5+ ♔g8 3 ♕xf7+ ♔h7 4 ♖d3! ♗xg5 5 ♖h3+ ♗h6 6 ♖xh6+! Black resigns.

47. 1...♗b2+! 2 ♔xb2 (2 ♘xb2 ♕c3+) 2...♖xb3+! 3 axb3 ♕xb3+ 4 ♔a1 ♘c2 mate. The game actually went 1...♖c3+ 2 ♔d2 ♖c2+, and Black nevertheless won.

48. 1...♗xg2+! 2 ♔xg2 ♕f2+ 3 ♔h1 ♖e1+! White resigns (4 ♕xe1 ♕f3 mate).

49. 1 ♗xh5! gxh5 2 ♕xh5 ♗e8 3 ♖f6! Black resigns.

TEST 8
Positions 50-55

---

50. 1 ♗b4!! ♕xb4 2 ♘xf6+ gxf6 3 ♕g6+ ♔h8 4 ♕xh6+ ♔g8 5 ♕g6+ ♔h8 6 ♕xf6+ ♔g8 7 ♖e3 Black resigns.

51. 1 ♗xg6! fxg6 2 ♖xg7+ ♔h8 3 ♕g4!! Black resigns.

52. 1 ♗xf4! ♘xf4 2 ♖xe7+!! Black resigns (2...♕xe7 3 ♕g8+ ♕f8 4 ♖xd8+).

53. 1 f5! exd5 2 ♕f4 ♖xc3 3 fxg6! ♘e5 4 gxf7 ♘xf7 5 ♖xg7! ♔xg7 6 ♖h7+! Black resigns.

54. 1...♗xd4+! 2 ♗xd4 ♖e1+!! White resigns.

55. 1...f3! 2 ♖xe3 ♘g4!! White resigns.

```
┌─────────────────────┐
│       TEST 9        │
│   Positions 56-61   │
└─────────────────────┘
```

56. 1...♘h5! 2 gxh5 ♖xh5+ 3 ♔g4 ♖g5+! (or 3...♕e2+ 4 ♕f3 ♕e6+ 5 ♔g3 ♕e1+ 6 ♕f2 ♖g5+) 4 ♔xg5 ♕f6+ 5 ♔g4 ♕f5+ 6 ♔h4 ♕h5 mate.

57. 1 ♘f5+! exf5 2 gxf5+ ♔h7 3 ♘g5+! hxg5 4 ♕h3+ ♔g8 5 ♖xg5+ ♔f8 6 ♕h8+ ♔e7 7 ♕f6+ ♔f8 8 ♕h6+ ♔e7 9 ♕d6+ Black resigns.

58. 1 ♘xh7! ♘xh7 2 ♖e3! (intending ♕xh7+!) 2...f6 3 ♗xg6 fxe5 4 ♖g3 ♖g7 (4...♔h8 5 ♗xh7 ♖xh7 6 ♕f8 mate) 5 ♗xh7+ ♔f7 6 ♖xg7+ ♘xg7 7 ♗g6+ Black resigns.

59. 1 ♘xd6! exd6 2 ♖xf7! ♖xf7 3 ♕xg6+ ♖g7 4 ♘f6+ ♕xf6 5 ♕xf6 Black resigns.

60. 1...♘e5! 2 ♕c7 ♖xh3! 3 dxe5 ♖h1+ 4 ♔xh1 ♕h4+ White resigns (5 ♔g1 ♕xf2+ and 6...♖h5 mate).

61. 1 ♘xe5! ♖xe5 (1...♗xe5 2 ♗xe5 ♖xe5 3 ♖xc6!) 2 ♗xe5 ♗xe5 3 ♖xc6! ♕xc6 4 ♕xf7+ ♔g7 5 ♖d7 ♖g8 6 ♘d5 Black resigns.

```
┌─────────────────────┐
│      TEST 10        │
│   Positions 62-67   │
└─────────────────────┘
```

62. 1 ♘f5! ♘cd3 2 ♖g7+! ♔h8 3 ♖c7! ♖xc7 4 ♕xd3! gxf5 Black resigns (in view of 5 ♗xe5+).

63. 1 ♘d4! exd4 2 ♕xd4+ ♔h6 3 ♖d7 ♕b1+ 4 ♔h2 ♖xf2 5 ♕e3+ g5 6 ♕h3+ ♔g6 7 ♕h7+ ♔f6 8 ♕g7+ ♔e6 9 ♕e7+ Black resigns.

64. 1 ♕c4! ♖e7 2 ♘xf7! ♖xf7 3 ♘xd6! ♕xd6 4 ♕xf7+! Black resigns.

65. 1 ♘xh6+! gxh6 2 ♖g4+! ♔h8 3 ♘xd5! Black resigns (3...♗xd5 4 ♕h7 mate!).

66. 1...♘xh2! 2 d7 ♗xd7 3 ♔xh2 ♕h4+ 4 ♔g1 ♘g4 5 ♕d6 ♕xf2+ 6 ♔h1 ♖b6! White resigns (7 ♕f4 ♕h4+ 8 ♔g1 ♖f6 9 ♕c7 ♕f2+ 10 ♔h1 ♖f5 and wins).

67. 1...♘xh4! 2 ♘f4 (2 gxh4 ♖xe6 3 ♕xf5 ♖g6+ 4 ♔h2 ♕xh4+ 5 ♕h3 ♕f4+ 6 ♔h1 ♖h6 and wins) 2...♖g5 3 ♕d7 (3 ♕h3 ♘f3+ 4 ♔g2 ♕c6 5 ♘d5 ♖xd5! 6 cxd5 ♕xd5 and wins) 3...♘f3+ 4 ♔g2 ♕h2+! 5 ♔xf3 ♖e3+! White resigns (6 fxe3 ♕xg3+ and ...♕xe3 mate).

TEST 11
Positions 68-73

68. 1 ♖hg1! ♗d4 2 ♖xg7! ♗xe3+ 3 ♕xe3 ♘f6 4 ♕g5 ♖ad8 5 ♖g1! Black resigns (5 ♖xd8 ♕xd8 6 ♕xf6! also wins).

69. 1 ♘xf5+! ♔h8 2 ♖xe4! ♘d7 (2...gxf5 3 ♖e8+ ♖xe8 4 ♖xe8+ ♔g7 5 ♕g5+ ♔f7 6 ♕g8+ ♔f6 7 ♖e6 mate) 3 ♕h6! ♖g8 (3...gxf5 4 ♖e7 and wins) 4 ♕xh7+!! Black resigns.

70. 1 ♘f6+! gxf6 (1...♔h8 2 ♕h5 with a strong attack; in particular 3 ♕xh6+ and 4 ♘e8+ is threatened) 2 ♕g4+ ♔h7 3 ♗e4+ f5 4 ♗xf5+! exf5 5 ♕xf5+ ♔g8 6 ♕f6 ♖d4!? 7 ♖xd4 ♘e5 8 ♖g4+ ♘g6 9 ♕h8 mate.

71. 1 ♖xf7! ♗xe5 2 ♖xg7+!! ♔f8 (2...♔h8 3 ♖f7!, or 2...♔xg7 3 ♕g5+ ♔f7 4 ♗xe5 and wins) 3 ♕h6! ♗xb2 4 ♖xh7+ Black resigns.

72. 1 ♘xe6! ♖g8 2 ♕h4+ ♔xe6 3 ♖de1+ ♔d7 4 ♕e7+ ♔c8 5 ♖f8+ ♖xf8 6 ♕xf8+ ♔c7 7 ♕xa8 Black resigns.

73. 1...♘xh4+! 2 ♔h2 ♖h1+! White resigns (or 2...♕h3+!).

TEST 12
Positions 74-79

74. 1 ♘e4! ♘xe4 2 ♖d3! ♗d7 3 ♖xc3 ♘xc3 4 ♗d3 Black resigns.

75. 1...♘axc3! 2 bxc3 ♗xc3+ 3 ♗b2 ♖c4 4 ♕f3 ♗xb2+ 5 ♔xb2 ♖c2+! 6 ♔xc2 ♕xa2+ 7 ♔d3 ♕c4+ White resigns.

76. 1 ♘xf7! ♔xf7 2 ♘g5+ ♔g8 (2...♔f6 3 ♕f3+! ♔xg5 4 ♕f4+ ♔h5 5 ♗e2 mate) 3 ♗xc7! ♕xc7 4 ♕b3+ e6 5 ♖xe6 Black resigns.

77. 1 ♕xa7!! c6 2 ♗f4 ♗d6 3 ♕a8+ ♔c7 4 ♘b5+! ♔b6 5 ♕a7+! ♔xb5 6 a4+ Black resigns (6...♔b4 7 ♕b6 mate).

78. 1 ♘xf7! ♖xf7 2 ♕a7! Black resigns (2...♖bf8 3 ♕xf7+! ♖xf7 4 ♖d8+).

79. 1...♘xg2! 2 ♔xg2 ♘f5 3 ♕g5 h6 4 ♕f6 ♖xd2 White resigns.

TEST 13
Positions 80-89

80. 1...b5! 2 ♕xb5 ♖ab8! 3 ♕xc6 ♕xa3! White resigns.

81. 1 e5!! fxe5 2 ♘fxe5! ♘xe5 3 ♘xe5 ♖f8 4 ♘xd7! ♖xf2 5 ♖fxf2 ♖d8 6 ♖e7 ♕g6 7 ♖f5! ♖e8 8 ♖e6! Black resigns.

82. 1 c6! bxc6 2 ♗xg7! ♕xg7 3 ♗a6+ ♔d8 4 dxc6 ♖e7 5 ♖d2 f5 6 ♕b3! Black resigns.

83. 1 e5! fxe5 (1...♕xe5? 2 ♘xc8+; 1...♘xe5 2 ♘e4 ♕c7 3 ♕b4+) 2 ♕g5+ f6 3 ♕g8! ♗b7 4 ♘f5+! exf5 5 ♕g7+ ♔e8 6 ♗h5+ Black resigns.

84. 1 d5! c5 (1...exd5 2 ♘xb6!) 2 ♘xb6! Black resigns.

85. 1...g5+! 2 fxg5 hxg5+! 3 ♔h5 ♕xh3+!! 4 ♕xh3 ♔g7! White resigns.

86. 1...exd3! 2 ♗a7 ♖xb7! 3 ♖xb7 d2! 4 ♖xd7 ♖xd7 Draw agreed.

87. 1 ♔e4! (1 ♔d4? a5! 2 ♔c3 ♔e6 3 ♔d4 ♔e7 =) 1...♔e6 (1...a5 2 ♔d4! ♔e6 3 ♔c5) 2 ♔d4 ♔e7 3 ♔c3 ♔e6 4 ♔b4! ♔e7 5 ♔a5 c3 6 c7 ♔d7 7 ♔b6 c2 8 e6+ Black resigns.

88. 1 ♕xf7+! Black resigns.

89. 1 ♔e3? (1 a4! ♔d6 2 a5 c4 3 a6! ♔c5 4 d6! ♔xd6 5 b6 and wins) 1...♔d6 2 ♔e4 c4 3 a4 c3 4 ♔d3 ♔xd5 White resigns.

TEST 14
Positions 90-96

90. 1...♕xc3! and wins. The game went 1...♖xg7? 2 ♖xg7+ ♔h6 3 ♖g8 ♔h7 4 ♖8g7+ Draw agreed.

91. 1 ♘xh6! ♗f6 (1...♘xh6 2 ♕g5+ ♔h7 3 f6 ♗xf2+ 4 ♔xf2 ♕f5+ 5 ♕xf5+ ♘xf5 6 ♗c2 ♔g6 7 g4 and wins) 2 ♗xf7! Black resigns.

92. 1...f3! 2 ♕xe8 fxg2+! 3 ♗xf8 gxh1=♘+ White resigns (4 ♔g1 ♗d4+ and wins).

93. 1 ♖xe7! ♕xe7 2 ♖e1 ♕d8 3 ♕h6 ♖g8 4 ♘xh7! ♗xh7 5 ♖e8!! Black resigns (5...♕h4 6 ♕g7 mate).

94. 1 ♕xe6+!! ♔xe6 2 ♗c4+ ♔f5 3 ♖d5+ ♘e5 4 ♖xe5+! ♔xe5 5 ♖e1+ ♔f4 (5...♔f5 6 ♗d3+ and wins) 6 g3+ ♔g4 7 ♗e2+ ♔h3 8 f3! Black resigns.

95. 1 ♖h8+! ♘xh8 2 ♔c6! ♖xd5 3 ♖b8+! ♔xb8 Draw agreed.

96. 1...♕xd5! 2 ♖xd1 ♗xa4 3 ♕xa4 ♕d2! White resigns.

Index of Players